Devotions With a Friend

Kenneth E. Tatum

Editing / Interior Book Design & Layout / Book Cover Design
CBM Christian Book Editing
www.christian-book-editing.com

Cover photo by Priscilla Du Preez on Unsplash

Printed in the United States of America

ENDORSEMENTS

Devotions with a Friend is comfortable reading, like discussing God's ways with an old friend; not like being lectured or made to feel "sinful". Rather, they assisted me in recognizing God's presence and actions and how I could become closer to God. The humor is refreshing.

I found myself returning to different articles when I realized I had encountered exactly what the author was describing. The memorable analogies and comparisons remain in my mind as memory "assists" to help me do God's work.

Mary McC.

I have enjoyed reading (the) devotions. They are longer than the typical one-page devotions. Questions made me stop and ponder about His Word and my life. I like the title *Devotions With a Friend*.

Kathy H.

Ken's writing is personable and easy to read and follow. You can tell he loves Jesus and wants his readers to draw closer to the Lord.

Alice W.

I think this is a wonderful book, thoughtful, interesting, very readable.

Kathy McK.

Dedication: To my sweet & patient Diane, the real writer in the family, without whom this volume would never have come to be!

Table of Contents:

An Introduction: *To the Reader*

What you will find on the following pages are thoughts that God has brought to my mind over quite a few years. Some thoughts came to me during countless hours of study and preparation for teaching an adult Bible study class. Some came as I was listening to sermons and lessons from one of my pastors or teachers. Some came from, or during, classes on the beliefs of other religions. But all came to me as I was going about daily life, trying to be a good witness to others of God's work in my life, even though often not fully succeeding at this task. The point is that God is continually trying to speak to us. Whether we are listening or not is up to us. I strongly suspect He has had many more things to say to me of which I have never even been aware. However, these thoughts came during times when I was actively trying to hear His voice, and I would like to share them with you.

These writings are not meant to be five minute "thought for the day" devotions. Those types of devotions can be of great value for when we are rushing to get breakfast on the table, kids ready for school, lunches packed, and frantically trying to get to work on time. They can help us get our attitudes focused on remembering who we belong to and point us mentally toward eternal viewpoints. But we also need to spend other, more thoughtful times meditating on what our Father wants to say to us, while also searching Scriptures for spiritual meat that helps our long-term spiritual growth. So, please, don't try to read these too quickly, hoping to squeeze it in as you dash about. My perspectives are possible responses to particular verses that may not be the final answers to your particular life situation. Yes, they may be, but also, maybe not. Instead, they may actually be gentle nudges that get you thinking about a particular passage in a new light. Try to meditate on the verses and see if my life experiences reflect yours. Then look for direct applications to your own life of the conclusions you finally reach.

I hope you, the reader, see these writings not as great theological treatises, but rather as simply expressions from another person on God's earth trying to live as one of His children. I am no great wise man, have not spent years in seminary, or retreated to a monastery to contemplate the mysteries of the universe. My suggestion is to read these brief notes sitting at your breakfast table with your favorite coffee or tea beverage in-hand or in the evening in your favorite easy chair as you rest from another busy day. Think of them as having a conversation with a close friend who is going through trials and stresses similar to yours. Spend a few minutes contemplating the scriptures referenced. Then realize one simple truth, please. If God can speak to a very imperfect me, then He can speak to you, as well. Not only can, but wants to, and will. Please listen for His voice, just as I have tried to.

Twenty-one articles are included in this volume. A routine that suits your needs and daily schedules might be every day for three weeks or maybe every weekday for four weeks, or even, if the workweek is too busy, only on Saturday and Sunday. But remember, while scheduling time with God is a great spiritual discipline, the most important thing is that you DO spend time with Him.

Now may our Lord bless you and keep you.

Ken T.

GRACE

Ephesians 2:8 *⁸For it is by grace you have been saved, through faith—and this is not from yourselves, it is the gift of God*

2 Corinthians 8:9 *⁹For you know the grace of our Lord Jesus Christ, that though he was rich, yet for your sake he became poor, so that you through his poverty might become rich.*

If there is one Christian spiritual concept that I don't really understand, it's grace. Now I know you are thinking, whoa! Grace is fundamental to Christianity. If you don't understand grace, then what do you understand? Or, if you don't grasp the idea of grace, can you even be a Christian?

But think about it. Does grace make any sense whatsoever? From a human perspective, grace is so far beyond reason that it's practically nonsense. I know we do sometimes show grace in our daily lives. Our kids do something they shouldn't do; and we forgive them, letting them off with some light punishment. Maybe a friend we have had for years betrays us at an inopportune time; but because of our years together, we try to forget it. Or a boss or co-worker takes advantage of us, and we just shake our heads and say it will be alright. Next time will be different, we think. There's no need to be vengeful now.

But are those occasions really instances of grace? Or are they just times when we are too tired or lazy to exact the punishment deserved?

Or too cowed by what the other party might do in return? Or too distracted by other, more pressing issues? In other words, are we really offering grace, or is something else driving our actions? Why would God offer us grace? Let's look at some concepts and ideas about grace.

You may know the **GRACE** acronym that has been touted for years. **G**od's **R**iches **A**t **C**hrist's **E**xpense. Remembering that is a good way to keep the idea of grace in our thoughts daily, but what are God's riches? I have a riding mower in my garage that I really like a lot. Going back, at my age, to pushing a hand mower would be awful! I remember when I realized that I could afford to buy that tractor. It never would have crossed my mind in earlier years while we were raising our kids and paying for our houses on much smaller salaries. I felt almost rich (and glad my wife gave me permission). But is that what God's riches are like?

I'm sure you are now shaking your head vigorously side-to-side. Of course not. The Bible tells us the cattle on a thousand hills are His. So, one small tractor is trivial. But, also, isn't the cattle on a thousand hills also trivial to Him? I think we all realize that "things" do not constitute God's riches, just like our most truly valuable possessions are not things.

The acronym's concept is not wrong, but rather our understanding of the word "riches" is poor. The Apostle Paul had to admit he didn't understand it any better than we do. In ***Romans 11:33*** he said, *"Oh,* *the depth of the riches of the wisdom and knowledge of God! How unsearchable his judgments, and his paths beyond tracing out!"* He used the term unsearchable to illustrate how little he understood God's riches. While we might think of looking up at some tremendous pile of riches like a dragon's hoard, Paul thought of looking down into unsearchable depths. Apparently to him it was not the immense height of the pile, but rather the depth or the source from which it all sprang that amazed him. Regardless of how much he saw, he knew that there would always be more rising up. The source of it all was truly unknowable. So, if you don't comprehend God's riches, you are in good company.

But is grace just about getting riches? That sounds a little selfish. Maybe it's not about getting more than we deserve, but receiving less than we deserve. What do we deserve? What do I deserve? As I look at my life, I know it's not much good. Most of my "deserving" is in the negative sense. Like when I know something is wrong, but I do it anyway. Or when I know God is telling me something to do and I ignore Him. What about the times I just react on my own without considering God at all? What do I deserve then?

I have just recently watched two TV shows about second chances; one modern show from 2020 and a second "vintage" rerun from the 1990s. In both shows, characters realized that they should treat another person differently than they had previously, and probably not the way the person deserved to be treated. Is that grace? Maybe, but is it God's grace? I can say from frequent personal experience that God has given me second chances, third chances, fourth, fifth, sixth, etc. Well, I suspect you get the idea. When I grant someone a second chance, that's good, but when God grants me a 237th chance, that's just unbelievable? Or, to use Paul's term again, unsearchable!

It is said there are five questions that beg for answers in nearly every circumstance: who, what, when, where, and why. The who is obvious: the Almighty God of all the Universe. The what is forgiveness offered for any and all of my sins. When was during the death and resurrection of Jesus, *circa* A.D. 30. Where is during my daily walk on this world that God made. But the why? I know God loves me, but THAT much? Amazing.

Now that I think about it, maybe it's not the concept of grace I don't understand, but rather that God loves me enough to grant me that much grace. Asked if he had been born again, author Frederick Buechner reputedly replied: "Let me tell you something, I have been born again, and again, and again." He was describing multiple experiences of God's grace. How much did God love Buechner? How much does He love me? You? Let's just say a lot, and leave it at that!

Prayer Emphasis: *Lord, thank you for your grace in my life. I know I will never understand it completely, but through it you have made me into a new creation.*

THE GREAT CHOREOGRAPHER

2 Corinthians 9:10 *[10] Now he who supplies seed to the sower and bread for food will also supply and increase your store of seed and will enlarge the harvest of your righteousness.*

1 Peter 4:11 *[11] If anyone speaks, they should do so as one who speaks the very words of God. If anyone serves, they should do so with the strength God provides, so that in all things God may be praised through Jesus Christ. To him be the glory and the power for ever and ever. Amen.*

Do you enjoy going to the movies? My wife and I do. Shortly after we were married, we babysat for some friends and took three small girls to see *"The Muppet Movie"* where we started a new tradition. We sat through the entire credits at the end *(mainly to keep from losing any of the girls in the crowd)* and we're glad we did. We got to see Animal appear, filling the entire screen, telling us to "Go Home!" That tradition has been a special fun activity just for us.

But sometimes, particularly for the recent big epic adventure movies, the credits are pretty lengthy. Oftentimes we are the only people left in the theatre by the credits' end. It takes an awful lot of people to make a movie these days: producers, costume designers, electricians, painters, animators, and even grips. Of course, who really knows what a grip is!

We like to see live plays, as well. We saw a production of **Les Misérables** that was produced in off-Broadway fashion with very minimal sets. In one scene the actors ran across loose planks to produce the desired sound effects! I suspect the credit roll at play-end was much, much shorter than most movies.

In ancient Greece one person usually served as the provider of everything the actors required. He was the Choreographer, the director who supplied what the actors and singers needed. I suspect he was a busy man, the essential link from written script to live performance.

In the two passages above, the words *"supply"* and *"provide"* are verb forms of the Greek word *"chorāgeo" (transliterated from Greek).* Note who the one doing the supplying is. In First Peter, God is named explicitly; and in Second Corinthians, He is the giver of our daily bread. In the Second Corinthians verse, the word *"supplies"* translates the same Greek word with an added prefix which emphasizes action. In other words, when God supplies, He is actively involved. He does not just send a relief truck of supplies or a delivery from the grocery via some angel. He is the one out on the streets driving the van and getting out to bring it into your house.

What kinds of supply does God give? The first verse mentions bread for food, for which The Lord's Model Prayer tells us we should ask daily. It also describes the delivery of resources for daily activities *(seed for the sower).* But God doesn't just give resources for the moment. He continues to increase our larder of supplies to the point at which the final product from those resources is better than could be imagined!

In First Peter, two specific activities of people are given: speaking and serving. The speaking is not just day-to-day, "I think the Steelers will win," conversations, but rather speaking God's words. It's worth noting that even, "The Steelers will win," can be God's words if He is directing someone to say them. Maybe that could be a conversation starter for growing a friendship, or maybe it's an opening for a deeper conversation about how we can win in real life.

Similarly, when someone serves others, it should not be done under their own power, but with the strength the great Choreographer (God) gives. In either case, speaking or serving, there needs to be one goal: bringing praise to God. Otherwise, what is done or said is purely selfish. If someone is able to do or say something meaningful or useful, with someone else's strength, shouldn't the original source of that ability receive the credit?

Do you need strength for some activity? Is that activity God-inspired? Maybe it's telling someone why your hope comes from a risen Lord. Maybe it's how prayer works. Or maybe it's taking a meal to an out-of-work neighbor you have just met. Maybe you DO need to talk about the Steelers versus the Packers.   Will God receive recognition and praise for what is accomplished? Tell them how Jesus brings you joy, even in the midst of a troubled world.   Are you frantically trying to do it within your own power, or do you recognize the need for an inexhaustible supply of resources? If so, there is a great Choreographer just waiting in the wings to give you what you need.

So, what kind of production do you think God has planned for your life? Is it a grand epic adventure with a huge cast of support staff? Will the credits at the end of your life be 10-15 minutes long? Or will it be like a Greek play where the credits have one name? I am not saying we should not work together as a Christian family, but I do believe that however many actors are involved, one Choreographer is all that is required!

Prayer Emphasis: *Lord, when you call upon me to act for You, I must remember to not do so in my own power. Thank you for the bounty of your supply.*

GOOD KING, BAD KING, GOOD KING, ... ?

<u>**2 Chronicles 33:1-2**</u>   *1 Manasseh was twelve years old when he became king, and he reigned in Jerusalem fifty-five years. 2 He did evil in the eyes of the Lord, following the detestable practices of the nations the Lord had driven out before the Israelites.*

And another description of Manasseh, many years later:

<u>**2 Chronicles 33:12**</u>   *12 In his distress he sought the favor of the Lord his God and humbled himself greatly before the God of his ancestors.*

In my day job as an engineer and scientist, I learned over the years that the entire physical world is connected. I studied the flow of gases, e.g., air, around many things. In fact, my co-workers and I tried to compute where the gas would go, when it would move, and how fast it would go, by solving, what looks like to most people, a fairly complex set of equations. To do so requires some pretty big and fast computers. When I first started as an engineer, we didn't have the powerful computers of today. We thought they were fast at the time but didn't have any idea what would exist years later. So back then, we settled for solving a very simplified approximation to those complex equations, one equation only. And we thought we got some good results by doing so. Boy, were we wrong!

Well, not really. Now we can do so much more, however. We have shown over and over that to really understand God's magnificent world we must solve highly complex systems of equations. The movement of air is coupled to the structure it is moving around, which is coupled to the material the structure is made of, and depends on the way it is supported, which …?

Okay, I suspect you get the point. But are physical processes the only parts of our world which are connected?

Take humans, for example. Are we connected? Does one person's actions affect others? Can our actions influence someone else? Does the action of another affect us? Can we change our actions to affect another in a different way? Let's look at one instance in the Old Testament to get answers.

King Manasseh is usually known as one of the worst of all Judah's rulers. He rebuilt idol altars, he worshipped the planets and stars, and he desecrated God's Temple in Jerusalem. But he was the son of King Hezekiah, often touted as one of the best kings of Judah. How could that happen? Obviously, Hezekiah had no influence on Manasseh. Correct? Or did he?

Hezekiah reigned very well for many years. He re-opened the Temple after many years of neglect. He reinitiated major times of corporate worship and invited the nation to renew their commitments to God. He destroyed pagan idols and led in prayer for defense of the nation against a seemingly invincible enemy.

But in later years he faced a health crisis, for which he prayed to God for relief. God answered his prayer and gave him fifteen more years of life. During these last fifteen years, however, Scripture tells us he became quite proud (*2 Chronicles 32:24-25*). Was his pride not just an internal thing, unrelated to other people?

Manasseh became the new king when Hezekiah died, at the tender age of twelve. What do you think Manasseh saw in his father as he grew during those twelve highly impressionable years? Prayer and worship? Caring for God's people? Or excessive pride? It would seem the latter. Regardless of Hezekiah's many good deeds years before, Manasseh learned pride, not compassion for others. He became a very bad king.

He undid much of the good that Hezekiah accomplished in his earlier years. However, since nothing is impossible with God, Manasseh probably startled the nation by actually hearing God speak to him. It took a lot to get his attention, but God did it, and *2 Chronicles 33:12* tells us he rejected Hezekiah's example of pride and humbled himself before God. In the last few years of his reign he attempted to undo much of the evil he had initiated. So, end of story. Right?

No, not quite. What about his son, Amon, who succeeded Manasseh? Amon was twenty-two when he became king. His impressionable years were most likely during Manasseh's reign of evil and Amon learned well. During his brief two years as king he repeated the evil of Manasseh's doings and did not humble himself before the Lord. It was so bad that his own servants assassinated him. Again, end of story. Right? Check out the next king.

Josiah was only eight years old when he succeeded Amon. So his first six years of life were during Manasseh's "good" years. Amon learned from Manasseh's evil. What did Josiah learn from his grandfather Manasseh? What kind of king was Josiah? **Second Chronicles 34:2** tells us: *"He did what was right in the eyes of the Lord and followed the ways of his father David, not turning aside to the right or to the left."* He did not repeat his father Amon's evil, but rather learned good from his grandfather Manasseh.

What does all this, maybe tedious, history tell us? Are our actions interconnected? Do our actions affect those around us? It certainly appears to have in this Old Testament time. In particular, our actions have a very strong influence on impressionable small children. This effect is not limited to parents but can also result from the teaching of grandparents. We know our roles as parents in teaching our children, but do we also recognize our corresponding roles as grandparents?

Yes, my scientific studies taught me our physical world is highly connected. But our personal worlds are connected as well. Let us learn from Hezekiah, Manasseh, Amon, and Josiah that we do influence others, even when we don't see it, or think others are watching. The Bible is a book about relationships. Let's think long and hard about ours.

Prayer Emphasis: *Lord, grant me discernment to see how my actions affect others, and develop within me the qualities that have positive effects.*

"DRY BONES": A MYSTICAL VISION

<u>Ezekiel 37:1-14</u>   *¹ The hand of the Lord was on me, and he brought me out by the Spirit of the Lord and set me in the middle of a valley; it was full of bones. ² He led me back and forth among them, and I saw a great many bones on the floor of the valley, bones that were very dry. ³ He asked me, "Son of man, can these bones live?"*

I said, "Sovereign Lord, you alone know."

⁴ Then he said to me, "Prophesy to these bones and say to them, 'Dry bones, hear the word of the Lord! ⁵ This is what the Sovereign Lord says to these bones: I will make breath enter you, and you will come to life. ⁶ I will attach tendons to you and make flesh come upon you and cover you with skin; I will put breath in you, and you will come to life. Then you will know that I am the Lord.'"

⁷ So I prophesied as I was commanded. And as I was prophesying, there was a noise, a rattling sound, and the bones came together, bone to bone. ⁸ I looked, and tendons and flesh appeared on them and skin covered them, but there was no breath in them.

⁹ Then he said to me, "Prophesy to the breath; prophesy, son of man, and say to it, 'This is what the Sovereign Lord says: Come, breath, from the four winds and breathe into these slain, that they may live.'" ¹⁰ So I prophesied as he commanded me, and breath entered them; they came to life and stood up on their feet—a vast army.

¹¹ Then he said to me: "Son of man, these bones are the people of Israel. They say, 'Our bones are dried up and our hope is gone; we are cut off.' ¹² Therefore prophesy and say to them: 'This is what the Sovereign LORD says: My people, I am going to open your graves and bring you up from them; I will bring you back to the land of Israel. ¹³ Then you, my people, will know that I am the LORD, when I open your graves and bring you up from them. ¹⁴ I will put my Spirit in you and you will live, and I will settle you in your own land. Then you will know that I the LORD have spoken, and I have done it, declares the LORD.'"

Ezekiel's mystical vision of a valley filled with long-dead bones is one of the most spectacular of the entire Bible. The reader is impressed immediately with the desolation and hopelessness of the situation. Most of us do not like cemeteries anyway, but being confronted with vast numbers of bones simply scattered about on the ground is more than any of us would want to see. How could anything positive be gleaned from such a sight?

But, the good, even great news, is that what is hopeless to us finite, mortal humans is child's play to God. As Jesus told His disciples, *"...with God all things are possible"* **(Matthew 19:26)**. As Ezekiel soon discovers, God can take those bones and reassemble them into not only individual persons, but assemble the persons into a mighty (but still dead) army. Then, just to complete the point, God finishes His work by breathing life into them. One more reminder that even life itself is a gift from God! What an awesome image of the eternal God's power! When we are feeling truly hopeless we have a God who is not only always in complete control, but also has the power to change everything and to even bring good out of death.

There you have it. The lesson from this vision of the valley of dry bones is the power of God to overcome anything. Even the hopelessness of the Jews' exile to a faraway land is not too much for Him.

So, that's it. Good Bible lesson, short, sweet, and to the point. Right? Maybe, maybe not. Is God showing us something else in this desolate valley?

Is everything always what it seems at first glance? Ezekiel was pretty sure he was looking at a place of desolation. Most of the Israelites had seen a plentiful land with their eyes when they spied out Canaan, but saw only giants and huge fortresses with their hearts. Which was it? Obviously it was both physically, but when Caleb looked through God's eyes he saw only the blessings of God's provision.

The Jews exiled to faraway Babylon saw the loss of everything they thought they had accomplished in conquering Canaan. Their homeland, their temple, all gone. How could they ever again be a proud nation? Did they not remember the mighty power God had exercised bringing them across the Red Sea, through long stretches of desert, overcoming fierce hostile nations, and bringing down the walls of Jericho? Were their eyes deceiving them, or were they just being realistic?

In the New Testament Jesus pointed out that our human vision can also deceive us the other way. The people saw the scribes and Pharisees as the ultimate men of God. They knew God's Scriptures backwards and forwards. Not only did they know those words they also made it a point to obey every one of them, right down to the smallest letter! So, when Jesus came He must have also thought them great. Right? No, He called them *"whitewashed tombs"* (**Matthew 23:27)**.

Why do we paint something white? Because it looks clean, pretty, and undefiled. We usually try to make our cemeteries look nice and pretty, and often new headstones are white. So, we say, "Isn't that a pretty place." But would you want to live there? I don't think so. It's a place for dead people and old bones. It may be neatly trimmed and freshly painted, but is it really a place we want to live in, or is it actually a cemetery? Is it a beautiful work of art? Or is it hiding something dreadful and hideous; maybe even merely covering scenes of death and desolation?

Can we trust our eyes to see what is really there? Are the eyes God gave us faulty?

The eyes God gave man originally were good (**Genesis 1:31** says that all He made was very good). But those eyes are physical ones for the physical world. They are limited to such and therefore can be deceived (**Luke 11:34**). God has far clearer sight. He looks within and not merely at the obvious (**1 Samuel 16:7**).

<u>Matthew 19:26</u>	*Jesus looked at them and said, "With man this is impossible, but with God all things are possible."*

<u>Matthew 23:27</u>	*"Woe to you, teachers of the law and Pharisees, you hypocrites! You are like whitewashed tombs, which look beautiful on the outside but on the inside are full of the bones of the dead and everything unclean.*

<u>Genesis 1:31</u>	*God saw all that he had made, and it was very good. And there was evening, and there was morning—the sixth day.*

<u>Luke 11:34</u>	*Your eye is the lamp of your body. When your eyes are healthy, your whole body also is full of light. But when they are unhealthy, your body also is full of darkness.*

<u>1 Samuel 16:7</u>	*But the LORD said to Samuel, "Do not look at his appearance or at the height of his stature, because I have rejected him; for God sees not as man sees, for man looks at the outward appearance, but the LORD looks at the heart."*

<u>Prayer Emphasis:</u>	*Lord, help me to see through your eyes, discerning the spiritual world, even as we live within the physical world You have given us.*

WHO IS MY ENEMY?

Matthew 5:43-45a *[43] "You have heard that it was said, 'Love your neighbor and hate your enemy.' [44] But I tell you, love your enemies and pray for those who persecute you, [45] that you may be children of your Father in heaven.*

In what we usually call the "Sermon on the Mount", Jesus frequently upended traditional thoughts on moral actions, thoughts, and perspectives. In the passage just quoted He went to an extreme of which I doubt anyone in His audience would have even dreamed. Many, if not most, in His Jewish audience would have known of the Old Testament command found in *Leviticus 19:18* to "love your neighbor". And I suspect many would have just assumed that the "hate your enemy" part of this "traditional" statement was also Biblical. We now know, of course, that it is not a quote from Scripture, but rather simply the natural human extrapolation to what we might want the Old Testament command to be. So we modern Christians breathe a sigh of relief and say, "Of course we are to love our neighbors and of course we should love our enemies." But do we ever go the next step in our thought processes and ask the hard question: Who does Jesus really mean by these categories of neighbor and enemy?

One expert in the Mosaic Law did ask the first half of this question. In *Luke 10* we read about an encounter with Jesus where he asked Jesus what he must do to inherit eternal life. Rather than answer him directly Jesus asked the man for his understanding. The expert immediately quoted the command to love the Lord your God with all your being and also the Leviticus passage of loving your neighbor. The man then asked Jesus the obvious question, "Who is my neighbor?" In response Jesus shared the famous parable of the Good Samaritan, presumably to show the man who his neighbor was.

As He finished His story Jesus asked the law expert a reverse question. Obviously Jesus wanted to find out if the man had truly understood and "gotten" the point! So, He asked the man if he now knew who his neighbor was. Correct? No, Jesus' question was not worded in the expected form. Instead He asked who "acted as" a neighbor, and not "who is" your neighbor. Why would Jesus not answer the man in a simple and straightforward manner?

I believe He was trying to change the man's thought process from defining everyone else as a specific type of person to determining what type of person he himself was. Which matters more? Who some individual is to me, or who I am to that individual? What category I place a person in, or how I treat the person? I cannot change that other individual, but I can change my own attitudes and actions toward that person. For me, the important point is how I live and act. Am I a neighbor?

But that answers only half of the pertinent questions. Just as Jesus said to love your neighbor, He also said to love your enemy. So, is it not also important to ask, "Who is my enemy?" How might Jesus answer that question? I won't presume to guess what parable He might tell to illustrate His meaning, but I can guess how He might word His question back to us at the end of the story. Would He ask, "Who then was the enemy of the main character?" Or would He ask, "Who acted as an enemy to others?"

The first question would fit within our natural human impulses to put people into nice, neat categories. But if Jesus discouraged us from placing people into a neighbor category, would He not do the same regarding enemies? I believe, more likely, that He would want us to ask ourselves, "Toward whom are we acting as an enemy?" "Who are we an enemy to?"

As with the neighbor question, the important detail is not the status of someone else, but rather the status of our own thoughts and actions. How am I treating another individual? Am I loving them, being compassionate for their hurts, and caring for their deep concerns? Or am I actively hating them? Disparaging them? Saying all manner of evil against them? Driving them away and pushing them into ghettos and slums of their native lands?

These days we hear a lot of talk from people who claim the name of Christ about the United States having many enemies. They name specific nations, people groups, or individuals. I will not speculate on whether any of these really are enemies. But Jesus said that if we really are children of God the Father, we are to love them anyway. And if love is actually a verb rather than a noun, then our love needs to be active. Calling them derogatory names and telling them to stay away is the opposite of love. In fact, Jesus directly addressed such things earlier in the Sermon, relating the "Do not murder" command to anger and name-calling (***Matthew 5:21-22***).

In short, the question to ask ourselves is, "Do we truly want to be children of the Father?" If so, we must love. Actively. Everyone. Is there a risk to doing this? Absolutely! But I believe Jesus Himself took the ultimate risk when He died for us. Dare we, His children, not imitate our Lord?

<u>Prayer Emphasis:</u>   *Lord, it is hard for me to love my enemies, but you loved me even when I was your enemy. Help me to not be an enemy, but to love those who might act as enemies to me.*

CHRISTIANITY: MASCULINE OR FEMININE?

<u>Mark 10:17-22</u> *[17] As Jesus started on his way, a man ran up to him and fell on his knees before him. "Good teacher," he asked, "what must I do to inherit eternal life?"*

[18] "Why do you call me good?" Jesus answered. "No one is good—except God alone. [19] You know the commandments: 'You shall not murder, you shall not commit adultery, you shall not steal, you shall not give false testimony, you shall not defraud, honor your father and mother.'[a]"

[20] "Teacher," he declared, "all these I have kept since I was a boy."

[21] Jesus looked at him and loved him. "One thing you lack," he said. "Go, sell everything you have and give to the poor, and you will have treasure in heaven. Then come, follow me."

[22] At this the man's face fell. He went away sad, because he had great wealth.

The following is probably directed more toward the guys than the gals, but I believe there is something here for all of us to learn. Look closely at the story from the gospel of Mark about the young rich man who desperately wanted to gain eternal life. Normally when we study this episode in Jesus' ministry, we talk about the need to sacrifice everything for Christ. He doesn't want just pieces and parts of us; He wants all of us or nothing. Or we talk about the potential idols in our lives that come between us and God. Those are very good studies and very true. But I think there is another issue that we need to explore to help primarily us guys understand what it means *(and takes)* to follow Jesus.

I have heard claims from several sources that Christianity has become a woman's religion. That it has become feminine and thus is a turn-off to men. The "love everyone" religion is just not a masculine thing to get involved with. Is all that talk really true?

I can't claim that some folks have not fostered this idea, or that in some churches that is not the appearance. But I do insist that true Christianity is not merely feminine. I think we can see that in this story of the rich young man.

I imagine everyone has heard stories from tribal cultures of how a young lad is expected to perform some "manly" act of bravery to prove that he is worthy of joining the cadre of tribal warriors and leaders. He may be expected to strike out on his own into unknown territory to kill a ferocious beast, or to survive for a period of time on his own without the help of his family or other associates. We may not have the same customs in our modern world, but don't we have similar concepts? Going on your first deer hunt? Re-building the engine of your first car? Converting that pile of lumber into a great-looking bookcase or workshop? Riding a motorbike cross-country? Quarterbacking the college team to the conference championship? A young man who has accomplished something like that is surely a man. I believe you can come up with other masculine feats to add to that short list. But, whatever the activity, the sure sign of maturing masculinity in any culture is the exercising of bravery or ability.

Now, back to the rich young man to whom Jesus was talking. What was it that Jesus really asked of him? Or, from the other perspective, what was the young man really asking? Wasn't it basically, "What feat of bravery can I do to gain eternal standing within God's kingdom?" Or, put another way, what masculine thing do I need to do to be considered grown up? (I doubt he was looking for a "cuddle an infant" type of activity!) Jesus replied by telling him to follow all the laws of the Jews that they had received from God. That, quite frankly, was an impressive assignment. But the young man was sure he had already done that and presumably knew that was not sufficient. So, what additional feat of manhood was required?

Since Jesus already knew what the answer to His first response would be, and because He really did want the man to gain eternal life (He loved him), He now decided it was time to give the real answer. "Give away everything you have, and then come, follow me." Now there is an act of bravery and masculinity, if ever I heard of one! Remember the picture of the would-be warrior heading out into the unknown carrying only his bow and arrows and maybe a knife? Here is Jesus calling this young man to leave everything behind, even his hypothetical "bow and knife"! Would it take an act of bravery to do that?

Isn't Jesus simply calling this fellow to do what he stated more distinctly in **Luke 9:23**? *"Deny yourself, take up your cross daily, and follow me."* Denying yourself can be interpreted as denying yourself the things of life, the things that you count on and that fill your life. Or, more precisely, denying your momentary desires, aspirations, and dreams so that you can then pick up the eternal desires and aspirations of God. In order for this young man to be granted citizenship in God's kingdom for eternity he needed to put aside the physical things and to accept spiritual things. Giving up all physical things for (visually) unseen spiritual concepts is the consummate call to demonstrate your manhood.

So, if this is a core concept in gaining eternal life in Christ, is Christianity a feminine religion? I think not. In fact, I would suggest the exact opposite appears to be true!

"But wait a minute," I hear the ladies in the audience saying, "if Christianity is a masculine religion, then what about us?" Is there no place for women and feminine characteristics in God's eternal kingdom? Of course there is a place. Note that I said this incident "appears" to show Christianity to be masculine. But actually it only shows that it is not necessarily feminine. Other episodes in the life of Christ show nurturing and compassionate aspects of Jesus' ministry, such as caring for the sick and the lame, restoring the dead son to the widow of Nain, and touching the deepest emotional needs of the woman at the Samaritan well.

You see, God is spirit, neither masculine nor feminine. We refer to the Father because that picture well illustrates the ways in which He cares for us. And Jesus came to Earth as a man in order to take our punishment as a human. There are only two choices and He had to choose one; He couldn't be both. Also, the most common Greek pronoun used for the Holy Spirit is of neuter gender, neither male nor female. So, what does that mean to us?

When we come to Christ for salvation He calls us to deny ourselves, as I said earlier, to put aside our earthly desires and aspirations. But He does NOT call us to deny ourselves of who we are, who He has made us to be, or the gifts and talents He has given us. If you have exceptional skills in repairing car engines He only calls you to change the direction in which you use that gift. No longer be lusting after building the super-charged muscle car so that you look good in front of your peers. Instead offer that gift back to the One who gave it to you in the first place. I am positive He knows how that gift can be used to benefit your brothers and sisters. Similarly, if you are a skilled nurse or an expert knitter, offer those skills to your Lord so that He can use them to His glory and in His ministry to His people.

So now we come back to my original question. Is Christianity a woman's religion? Can or should a man have anything to do with it? I believe the answer is yes, of course, to both questions. In fact, it is the ultimate act of manhood to give up all so that He can give you what truly is "all". And it is also the ultimate act of womanhood to proclaim Him as Lord and thus become the woman He really intends for you to be.

<u>Prayer Emphasis:</u>   *Lord, grow me to be the man or woman you want me to be, proclaiming you as Lord to all, and offering you all my life and service.*

ONE-WORD LESSONS

John 19:28   *Later, knowing that everything had now been finished, and so that Scripture would be fulfilled, Jesus said, "I am thirsty."*

John 19:30   *When he had received the drink, Jesus said, "It is finished." With that, he bowed his head and gave up his spirit.*

Matthew 28:6   *He is not here; he has risen, just as he said. Come and see the place where he lay.*

KA-POW! BAM! OUCH! CLANG! Do those words look (or sound) familiar? They probably do if you are a fan of the 1960's Batman TV show. Can't you see it now? You see KA-POW flashed across the screen and you immediately see in your mind Batman landing an uppercut on a bad guy's chin. You see OUCH on the screen and see Robin wincing from the fist of The Joker's henchman.

Great American literature? Spectacular cinematic presentation? No, not hardly. It's been described as "campy" and juvenile, but we loved it! The producers packed so much fun into a mere 30 minutes, and part of the reason was those one word flashes on-screen. We didn't have to see a thirty to forty minute fight scene to get full immersion into the storyline. One word was sufficient.

But that was fifty years ago, and we are much more sophisticated now. Our current TV shows, movies, and books are more cultured and mature. No one-word flashes for us; we want the full experience. Right?

Well, maybe not. Ever hear the word Jackpot? Bullseye? Eek! Beware! Do you know what is being communicated with those words? Of course, you do. While we often learn from hearing thirty to forty minute lectures or sermons or by reading 500 page books, sometimes the best lessons and information can be transmitted in a single word. Have you ever seen a child reaching upward in the kitchen and simply said "hot" to save him from serious pain?

I believe God has used that format to teach us some good lessons, as well. In these three verses God transmitted some powerful truths in a single word, although it is not obvious in most Bible translations. All of the verses contain modern English translations of single Greek words.

The Gospels record seven things Jesus said as He was dying on the cross, and two of them are single Greek words which are usually (and correctly) translated as multiple English words consisting of a subject and a verb. For example, the single word transliterated from Greek letters as *"dipsō"* becomes *"I thirst"*. And the Greek *"tetelestai"* becomes *"It is finished"*. But, just for a moment, consider the context of Jesus' statements. Jesus was up all night, tried and beaten, led from the Sanhedrin to Pilate to Herod and back to Pilate, paraded through the streets, and then nailed to the cross. I suspect at that point nobody would have spoken a grammatically well-constructed sentence. His one-word exclamation, **Thirsty!**, helps us fully understand the gravity of the situation.

Similarly, His second statement shows us what He was focused on. Again, there was no need for grammatical correctness. Similar to the Batman word-flashes, when Jesus declares **"Done!"** we know exactly what He meant. No need for elaborate sermons and explanations. God had come to Earth. The God-man had performed His mission, and God's plan was now complete. Nothing else was left for Jesus to accomplish. The Father would take over now. What more do we need Jesus to do for us?

But God is not through with His one-word declarations in the Gospels. When the angel appeared at the empty tomb on the first day of the week he had an important announcement to make to the first visitors. After acknowledging their desire and telling them not to fear, he simply says (in Greek) *"āgerthā"*, usually translated *"He has risen"*. A single word with eternal significance. The One they assumed dead was dead no longer. Death, the final end for all, was defeated, and no longer could cause any real damage. He was alive. Yes, the angel continued by offering evidence and giving further instructions. But the basic truth that everything had now been forever changed only required a single word: ***"Risen!"***.

Note that you don't hear the women saying, "What do you mean risen?", "How can this be?", or even "Quit fooling around, just tell us where to find him." They knew. Somehow, they just knew. No need to go to seminary to learn the theological nuances. No consulting a Concordance or Bible dictionary. They simply knew what the angel meant. And, further, they knew enough to go tell others, which they immediately did.

In every part of life from TED Talks, University lectures, YouTube, and Sunday sermons we have opportunities to learn important things, from how to receive email to how to perform open-heart surgery. These can be important lessons. But let us never underestimate the power of a single word. Thirsty. Finished. Risen!

Prayer Emphasis: *Lord, I praise you for the marvelous ways you speak to me. Whether it is a single word or a lengthy lecture, grant me spiritual ears with which to hear and comprehend.*

DOING SOMETHING STUPID

<u>**Acts 9:10-13**</u>   [10] In Damascus there was a disciple named Ananias. The Lord called to him in a vision, "Ananias!" "Yes, Lord," he answered.

[11] The Lord told him, "Go to the house of Judas on Straight Street and ask for a man from Tarsus named Saul, for he is praying. [12] In a vision he has seen a man named Ananias come and place his hands on him to restore his sight."

[13] "Lord," Ananias answered, "I have heard many reports about this man and all the harm he has done to your holy people in Jerusalem."

Have you ever been asked to do something that you knew was stupid? Like from your new acquaintance who asked you to pick him up in front of the Bank after he did a little *"business"* there, while he was pulling his stocking cap down over his face? Or maybe your childhood friend who talked you into going out on the narrow ledge over the big river? By the way, I did, despite knowing it was dumb, but fortunately, by God's grace, lived to write about it these fifty plus years later!

Why do we do those things, in spite of our better judgment? Are we just simply not thinking at all? Do we assume, "It'll never happen to me"? Or is it some kind of trust in the one requesting? Maybe we feel embarrassed if we don't, or feel like it's an obligation and not a request. You probably have your own reasons, but we have all done something like this at least once. One Biblical character, named Ananias, was told to do something that he thought was totally nonsensical, but he did it anyway.

Ananias may have felt like he was caught between a rock and a hard place. He heard his God tell him to do something that, as far as he knew then, sounded like suicide. Saul was not someone who a believer in Jesus wanted to see. Scripture refers to "murderous threats" coming from Saul's mouth, and apparently they were not idle threats; he had been making good on them. Of course, you and I know with 20/20 hindsight that God had just appeared to Saul, and forever changed him. But, Ananias did not have the luxury of hindsight. He evidently feared for his life to go and do what his Lord had said to do.

Now you might say, "But God appeared to him in a vision. That should have been satisfactory to him." How sure are you, no, how sure are we, that every dream or insight or vision we receive is a sure thing from God? In this technical twenty-first century, we doubt anything that seems to be supernatural or spirit-like! Yet we expect Ananias to just accept it as true and go. Granted, people in the first century AD were a lot more receptive to the concept of the spirit world than we are, but that included belief in demons as well as angels. I think it is only natural that Ananias would question this vision and command.

Fortunately for Ananias and for us, God did not strike him dead for questioning. Instead God simply repeated His command, adding His reasons for sending Ananias to visit Paul. God asks us to operate on faith, but He does not always require us to. He is willing to work with us where we are in our own spiritual journey. He told Ananias exactly what His plans for Saul were, and apparently expected Ananias to pass those plans on to Saul. In fact, God did not make any reference to possible suffering by Ananias, but instead referred only to suffering that this supposed enemy would undergo!

Yes, Ananias was fearful. He did question God's command. But he didn't stand around and argue. He heard, listened, and obeyed. I am sure he was still wondering what was going on right up to the time he entered Saul's room. But, I repeat, he went at God's command, even though it made no human sense at all. I am sure many of his acquaintances would have said, "Ananias, that's a stupid thing to do."

What has God asked us to do that seemed to be ridiculous, or against our better judgment? Did we do it anyway? Ananias could have said, "No, that doesn't make any sense. I must have heard God wrong, or that must not have really been God speaking." Jesus tells us in **John 15** that we must abide in Him in order to have a fruitful life. Abide means to live in, not just visit occasionally. When we live with someone daily, we recognize their voice. The only way that Ananias could have been sure this was God talking to him, and not some lure to do something dumb, was to have been abiding in Christ. He had to be connected to the true vine in order to bear fruit for His Lord.

What difference would it have made if he had not gone to Saul? Would our Christian faith of today be the same without the witness of a man later called Paul? This was a man who witnessed to much of the then-known western world, started churches all around the Mediterranean Sea, and wrote over half of the New Testament. Would we be missing anything in our understanding of God if we didn't have Paul's letters? What might be the difference if we decide that God "really didn't mean to ask that of me?" Would, or could, our disobedience mean that some future generation would miss the witness of another Paul? I don't know the answers to those questions, but do we (or I), want to take that chance? Wouldn't it be better to let an infinite, all-knowing God be the one to answer that question?

Prayer Emphasis: *Lord, please call me to act in ways that touch the lives of others for you, knowing your guidance will never steer me wrong.*

TRUE BELIEF

Mark 9:21-24 *[21] Jesus asked the boy's father, "How long has he been like this?"*

"From childhood," he answered. [22] "It has often thrown him into fire or water to kill him. But if you can do anything, take pity on us and help us."

[23] "'If you can'?" said Jesus. "Everything is possible for one who believes."

[24] Immediately the boy's father exclaimed, "I do believe; help me overcome my unbelief!"

What do people believe in these days? I presume most of you readers are well beyond believing in Santa Claus, the Easter Bunny, or the Tooth Fairy. But do we have other, more adult, images that are critical to us? We believe that one certain celebrity would never lie to us and that their detergent/shampoo/teeth-whitening product has got to be the one for us. We believe our late model SUV will certainly get us to the store or work or school. We believe our favorite political candidate is going to win it all.

Unfortunately, many times these beliefs are proven wrong, and our car does fail us. That politician runs afoul of an accusation from their past, and he quickly disappears from the scene. Or, worst of all, that cleaning product fails to get the grape juice stain out of that freshly laundered shirt, after we failed to keep close watch on our 4-year-old! After several of these failures we can easily become cynical and decide that nothing is deserving of our trust. There becomes nothing we can truly believe in.

For many reasons, true belief is tough for finite human beings. The healing of a son cursed with seizures from childhood must have seemed impossible to the father. Nothing showed him any reason to believe that his son could be healed. Yet, as a compassionate parent, he never gave up hope. He had heard of Jesus, and His healing ministry, so the father brought his son in the hope that the miraculous could indeed occur. As it so happened, Jesus was not present when the pair first arrived, and nine of the disciples received one of their many lessons on walking minute-by-minute, no, second-by-second, with the God of the Universe. Their faith was not yet sufficient, and the father must have despaired once more. Just like the highly-touted detergent that fails to get out the grape juice stain, these disciples were not up to the task at hand.

But, as Jesus is apt to do even today, he arrived just in the nick-of-time and asked what the commotion was all about. After mildly chastising His disciples, He sought to do what He came to Earth for: To seek relationships with His people. Compassionately, He spoke to the father, expressing concern for the child's illness.

The father responded as many of us would; he didn't want conversation, he wanted physical healing for his son. But unlike most of us, he also spoke candidly. He did not try to hide his feelings and be "politically correct." He admitted he did not totally understand Jesus. He did not yet have total faith that Jesus could heal, and he told Jesus so. His final plea was for Jesus to have mercy on both him and his son, if He was able! The father did not yet know what power Jesus had. Both father and son were suffering under the weight of the illness. Could Jesus heal?

To build the father's faith, Jesus declared that true belief is integrally connected to overcoming the impossible. Did the man have such faith?

Yes, the man replied, digging down into the very core of his being, he did have some belief. But he realized that even that might not be enough! He was a very wise man. In his despair at his own inadequacy, he threw himself totally upon Jesus' mercy. "Help me overcome my unbelief," is a cry we all need to make to God at some point during our lives. God knows we are not perfect; He made us! And fortunately, He is continuing to make us, and even re-make us. When we begin to realize and admit that our faith is limited at best, Jesus is always willing, and even anxious, to provide the help we need. If only we would be more honest with Him as this hero of the faith was. In the end, Jesus took the mustard-seed faith of this man, and grew it into a faith that can move mountains through the power of the One who made the mountains.

In the end, Jesus did heal the son, commanding the source of the illness to go away, though it did not do so quietly. To those gathered there, the cure may have seemed worse than the disease, but Jesus calmly touched the son and raised him to his feet, whole and well.

Mark tells us nothing more about the father and son, but I have to believe the dad now had a new understanding of belief. He now knew the impossible can be possible, but only with belief in the right person. Not the disciples, but Jesus. He also knew that God is always willing to bolster our weak belief. It is not our strength that matters, but God's.

The disciples were perplexed, however. By this time in Jesus' ministry they knew nothing was impossible, but they had yet to find the right power. That power comes only from God. Jesus told them that power comes only when they pray and stay connected to Him in faith (*John 15:5*). They, like us, must spend time talking with Him, believing His promises. Then, though our faith may be weak, we discover that God never is.

<u>Prayer Emphasis:</u>   *Lord, I believe you are Lord of Lords and King of Kings. Please help my unbelief.*

TEAMWORK: RAH, RAH, RAH

1 Corinthians 12:12-14   *12 Just as a body, though one, has many parts, but all its many parts form one body, so it is with Christ. 13 For we were all baptized by one Spirit so as to form one body—whether Jews or Gentiles, slave or free—and we were all given the one Spirit to drink. 14 Even so the body is not made up of one part but of many.*

As our kids grow and mature beyond the stages of blocks and toy cars, we have to look for more ways of exercising their new abilities. Wooden blocks and toy cars are great for a two to three-year-old, but not so much for a ten-year-old. To develop their muscles and dexterity they need new, more complex activities. Athletics and sporting endeavors often become the next opportunities for both physical and mental development.

At this point, however, parents have to make a choice. Do they steer their child into individual sports or team sports? Swimming is great exercise, as are ice skating and gymnastics. They can do wonders for the body, but do team sports offer additional benefits? T-ball and soccer help with coordination and agility, but they also teach kids how to be part of a team where doing well personally is only part of the whole picture. For the team to do well, each member contributes only a piece of the puzzle. The shortstop can make a great play, but the first baseman must catch the throw for the out. The defenseman can make a tremendous stop, but if the forwards do not control the ball downfield the team still cannot win.

One solution to this problem that many kids try initially is to do it all themselves. The shortstop catches the ball and runs to first rather than throwing. The defenseman makes the stop and then heads up field toward the goal. But the shortstop gets beat to first by the batter because of the distance from his or her shortstop position. The sturdy defenseman finds that there are nine or ten opposing players waiting and ready for him. If he had kicked the ball downfield, the receiving forward may have only had one or two opponents to get by.

Teamwork is essential for these soccer and baseball players. No one can do it all, but each one must do their own part. Everyone is asked to participate, and when one fails to contribute the team fails to win. Even in the worlds of swimming and gymnastics the athletes find that eventually they must become part of a team. They can spend many years honing their skills; but when they reach the Olympics, they discover that their country is credited not only with individual medals, but also team medals. Everywhere we look we are involved in team activities, even at our jobs in adulthood.

So, is there an analogy in this for our Christian lives? The Corinthians passage confirms that when we become Christians we are joining a team. The Corinthians passage calls it a body, the body of Christ. We become a part of the body when we claim Jesus as Lord and Savior and are immersed in the Holy Spirit. A body is a team, but even more so. Both have many parts which are integrally connected to one another. When one of those parts fails, either the team or the body suffers.

Subsequent verses in this twelfth chapter *(vv. 15 through 26)* discuss those body parts and how each one is essential, but none is more important than another. A foot and a hand are not to compete with one another, but should complement one another. The eye cannot tell the hand it is not needed just like the shortstop cannot tell the first baseman he is not needed. The toe is not necessarily the prettiest body part, but without it how stable would the body be? The toe should not want to be an eye. A very old *(and bad)* joke tells of how a toe wanted to be an eye, and God allowed it. But all the toe would ever see was the inside of a sock!

A body has all the parts needed to function as God has planned. Similarly, the body of Christ has all the parts required as God wants it to have *(v. 18)*. Not all the same part because that would not be a real body, but many discrete parts that form a complete body. What part of Christ's body are you?

Are you a teacher? If so, God has given you a spiritual gift of teaching, and that is an important function within the body. Are you a child care worker? Then God has gifted you with a spirit of nurturing. Are you a preacher? Then you have a gift of speaking. Pastors are given the gift of feeding and shepherding their flock. I can speak confidently of this because **verses 7-10** tell us the Spirit indwells and gifts every part of the body as He desires, all for the common good. If He called you to be an elbow, then He will give you the ability to be the very best elbow ever! The body of Christ functions best when all the elbows, kidneys, necks, ears, toes, and pinky fingers are functioning just as God has planned.

If you are a member of Christ's body, do you know what part you are? Do you compete with other parts so that people think your part is the most important, or do you do your best to support other parts so they can serve well? Be sure you ask God for wisdom to know your "part" and function. Then grab your ball glove and run onto the field. The first baseman will really need your contribution.

Prayer Emphasis: *Lord, I want to be a functioning part of your body. Show me where I can serve and thank you for the gifts you give to empower me.*

NOTE FROM A TREE HUGGER

<u>Psalms 1:1-3</u>   *¹ Blessed is the one who does not walk in step with the wicked or stand in the way that sinners take or sit in the company of mockers, ² but whose delight is in the law of the Lord, and who meditates on his law day and night. ³ That person is like a tree planted by streams of water, which yields its fruit in season and whose leaf does not wither — whatever they do prospers.*

I confess. I am a "tree hugger." I love trees. Having spent my first twelve years on a 50 acre farm, tilled by my grandparents who lived down the hill from us, I spent many a day wandering through the woods that covered much of that land. I played cowboys and Indians, recreated Tarzan TV shows, and pretended to explore strange new lands as a young man. Ahh, those were the days! The freedom and even comfort I got as I wandered through those woods is probably hard to explain to someone from a city background. It was so peaceful, and on hot summer days it felt so good to step in amidst those trees and be able to feel the cooling, gentle breeze envelop me. Yes, I often miss those experiences.

Even as an adult, however, I still love trees. We have planted numerous trees on our current property and my wife has commented several times about how she loves our "park-like" back yard. I am particularly proud of the four oak trees that have grown so tall and the bald cypress that has such a beautiful shape. We also have several maples, two oriental raintrees, and a redbud that has recently begun blooming beautifully in the spring.

Another tree I have enjoyed being around through my life is the sassafras, a unique tree that can have three differently shaped leaves on the same tree. These trees typically grow quickly to a nice size and shape. And, of course, tea made from the sassafras root is an added benefit!

I have tried transplanting these trees on several occasions, but always to no avail. You see, they typically require more water than most trees and are often found growing along the banks of streams in the southern U.S. Unless you have a substantial storm-water drainage ditch nearby *(or a leak in the water-supply line to your house)* most residential neighborhoods are not going to be adequate for the sassafras.

The opening verses of the Book of the Psalms are familiar to many and are often used to point out the dangers of getting too close to wicked and evil men. We are blessed by God when we do not allow the wicked to pull us along with them in their evil ways, or even just become comfortable in the presence of men and women that mock Godly ways. Instead of those behaviors, we should find our joy in seeking God's guidance and contemplating His words.

Those words should be obvious enough. Don't ride along with the bank robber as he heads for his next heist. Don't sit at the bar with the town drunk. Don't swap dirty jokes with the irreverent prankster you just met. Instead, go to church every Sunday. Read your Bible daily and pray every morning when you first wake up. When we get those actions down pat, then God will bless us.

But, in the words of the old Peggy Lee song (©1969), "Is that all there is?" Reading verses 1-2 without verse 3 might lead you to believe so. However, verse 3 tells us the rest of the story. Why are we blessed, and how? If we do those actions for the right reasons and in the right spirit, we become like the sassafras tree growing by the country stream. In "The Change" Steven Curtis Chapman (©1999) sings about having the Jesus bumper sticker and the outline of a fish stuck on his car. But he wonders where the change is in his life. That change is what happens when we delight in, and meditate on, God's words. Then we find God's Spirit living inside us.

The "how" of being blessed is receiving God's Spirit. Not going out and getting it, but having it given to us. The sassafras doesn't go out looking for water. It begins growing in the right place and the water is just there for it to suck out of the ground. A sassafras that tries to grow in the desert doesn't find that life-giving water. Similarly, a person who walks with wicked people and sits with mockers will not find God near, but when they seek to hear God's voice, He will make it heard.

The answer to the "why" question is found in ***John 15:8*** which tells us that our fruit brings glory to God. We don't serve in a soup kitchen for the homeless to gain fame or self-satisfaction. We do it to show people that God loves them. The credit must be given to the One who created that food, so that men and women are drawn to Him, the giver of all good gifts.

I don't know about you, but I would like to be like that lovely sassafras tree that never lacks for nourishment. It grows so green and pretty, and is continually reproducing itself and spreading like wildfire all up-and-down the bank of the life-giving water. When your life is over wouldn't you like affirmation from the greatest tree-hugger of all when He tells you, "Well done, good and faithful servant," not because of the things you did, but because of the tall, fruitful tree you have become?

John 15:8   ***By this my Father is glorified, that you bear much fruit and so prove to be my disciples.*** *(English Standard Version)*

Prayer Emphasis: *Lord, give me a desire to be with you daily and drink in your life-giving Spirit. I want to be a fruitful tree and be "hugged" by You.*

FREE TO DO WHAT?

Galatians 5:13   *[13] You, my brothers and sisters, were called to be free. But do not use your freedom to indulge the flesh; rather, serve one another humbly in love.*

1 Corinthians 9:19-23   *[19] Though I am free and belong to no one, I have made myself a slave to everyone, to win as many as possible. [20] To the Jews I became like a Jew, to win the Jews. To those under the law I became like one under the law (though I myself am not under the law), so as to win those under the law. [21] To those not having the law I became like one not having the law (though I am not free from God's law but am under Christ's law), so as to win those not having the law. [22] To the weak I became weak, to win the weak. I have become all things to all people so that by all possible means I might save some. [23] I do all this for the sake of the gospel, that I may share in its blessings.*

If you are a student of history, I suspect you have noticed one common thread in most major conflicts. That thread is the desire of one party or the other for freedom to live as they see fit. The Israelites fled Egypt to escape slavery, and fought the Canaanites to establish a homeland where they could live and worship as they desired. Centuries later they struggled to throw off the rule of the Romans. The Scots fought the English over several centuries for the right of self-rule. Of course, the American Revolution was our own greatest example of a struggle for freedom. But the desire for, and struggle for, freedom continues today and does not just involve wars.

No person wants to be controlled by someone else. Even under seemingly benevolent masters, eventually differences of opinion lead to longings for freedom and the right to make our own choices. We want "life, liberty, and the pursuit of *[our own]* happiness."

So, when we gain freedom, how do we use the freedom that we gain? For many the answer is "whatever I want to do." For others, it might be what I have to do to survive. For a third group, it might be to climb the ladder and be successful. More generous folk may say it will be to help others. But, regardless, we want to be in control of our actions.

Paul insisted that Christ called us to an environment where we were to be free. But he seemed to have a strange idea of freedom. The word usually translated as "serve" is a verb form of the Greek word for slave. In other words, he calls us to use our freedom to submit to one another as slaves. What a paradox! If I am a Christian, am I free, or am I not? Is becoming a Christian simply a matter of changing who my Master is? The answer is very simply, yes!

As a non-Christian, I was a slave to whatever desires and lusts were present within me; I wanted to indulge my sinful nature. As a Christian, God is changing me into someone who doesn't want those same things, but instead wants to love as God loves me. And God loved me by dying for me to set me free. As God develops the mind of Christ in me, my thoughts and desires are being steadily changed into those of Christ. We don't need a rigid set of laws to corral our actions.

So how did Paul serve others? To whom did he submit to being a slave? And why?

Paul was ethnically a Jew, so the first in his list was easy. Or was it? The Jews had many rituals and observances they practiced attempting to gain righteousness. Paul knew doing those things didn't necessarily get him closer to God, but he did them anyway. Doesn't that seem like a waste of his time?

More specifically, though he knew the Law was not the end-all that the Jews wanted it to be, he was happy to abide by those laws if the Jews would accept him. He did not want to be seen as a rebel and a sacrilegious person, to those who saw the law as crucial, by ignoring it. But he also wanted to show the Gentiles that the Jewish law, which was not their law, was not his guiding principle. A higher law, which they could have, was available to all men. Christ's law was to love God and to love their fellow man.

Finally, although Paul was a strong personality, he was also willing to live as if he were weak. By this he meant a spiritual weakness, maybe even being seen as a young immature Christian, if that would help him to have a relationship with those persons. So, freedom for him meant he was free even to the point of abasing himself. Does that sound like the freedom you have been reaching to gain?

Why would Paul apply his freedom in these ways? I believe it all goes back to his single-minded focus in life. When God called him on the Damascus Road, He also sent him. God changed his former focus of eliminating Christianity to one of spreading Christianity. His new desire was for everyone to gain the blessing of freedom in Christ that he now had.

God sent him to call others to spiritual freedom in Christ. Do you get that? God called Paul to be free and sent him to call others to freedom (and salvation), who were sent to call others also, and who were then sent to call even more! It didn't matter who those "others" were: Jews, law-abiders, law-breakers, strong or weak. Paul was willing, and even eager, to use his new-found freedom to bring salvation to them all. In this way he not only brought blessings to others, but also received more blessings himself.

Do you want to be free? If you have that freedom, what do you do with it? What people group does God want you to reach out to through your freedom? Are you willing to use your freedom to bring God's blessing to others and share in them yourself?

Prayer Emphasis: *Lord, thank you for the freedom you have given me in Christ. Show me how to use that freedom to share your blessings and joys with others.*

JUST WHAT DO YOU KNOW?

<u>John 14:3-9</u>   *³ And if I go and prepare a place for you, I will come back and take you to be with me that you also may be where I am. ⁴ You know the way to the place where I am going."*

⁵ Thomas said to him, "Lord, we don't know where you are going, so how can we know the way?"

⁶ Jesus answered, "I am the way and the truth and the life. No one comes to the Father except through me. ⁷ If you really know me, you will know my Father as well. From now on, you do know him and have seen him."

⁸ Philip said, "Lord, show us the Father and that will be enough for us."

⁹ Jesus answered: "Don't you know me, Philip, even after I have been among you such a long time? Anyone who has seen me has seen the Father. How can you say, 'Show us the Father'?"

Ahh, school days! Those wonderful days of our youth spent hanging out with our buds at the mall, showing our spirit at basketball and football games, band trips, prom, and running for class president. What a marvelous, relaxing time when we didn't have a care in the world. Oh, wait a moment. There was that minor issue of getting up early every morning and going off to spend 6-7 hours sitting in a classroom. But, of course, that was fun, too, wasn't it? We must all admit we really looked forward to that homework every night, the 8-10 page essays we were assigned, and the monotonous word problems from our math textbooks. Right? Well, maybe everything was not quite as rosy as we like to think.

So, what kept you going every morning so you could be subjected to all this hard labor, that is, besides the threat of the truant officer coming to find you? (Note, despite that threat I NEVER remember seeing one!) Was it the excitement of stashing all that great and useful knowledge inside your brain? Or love of fractions, or geometric proofs, that kept you going? I bet it was the sentence diagramming that did it (my English teacher wife's favorite torture).

One of my most vivid school memories was memorizing the multiplication tables. Over and over we wrote those tables (3rd grade, I believe). By the time the year was over I knew that $6 \times 7 = 42$. It was ground into my subconscious. I was equally sure I had wasted a lot of time doing those exercises. But, lo and behold, many years later working as an engineer I came to know that fact in a whole different way. The expression "6x7" became part of equations that determined how well airplanes flew and whether a wind tunnel worked as desired. I knew the fact in 3rd grade, but now I perceived the fact as important and necessary; it was now real to me. I suspect this is true in many other realms of knowledge. A medical student may hate memorizing the bones of the skeletal system, but when a patient of his asks why his back hurts, the now-practicing physician realizes where the pain originates.

Jesus told the disciples that they knew where He was going, but Thomas was not so sure. Two Greek words are translated "know" in this passage in most translations. One refers to simple facts we experience, such as the fact that 6x7=42 which I learned doing multiplication tables, over and over. The one used in verses 4 and 5, though, has the sense of perceiving something as fact. That is what I came to do as an engineer when I not only knew the fact of 6x7=42, but also perceived how it made a difference in my work. So, regardless of Jesus' assertion (**v4**), Thomas did not believe he had perceptual knowledge of where Jesus was going. In other words, despite the fact that Jesus had repeatedly told them what the future held, Thomas had not perceived the implications and, thus, did not know what to do next.

In verse 6 Jesus presented to them the fundamental facts of the case. Similar to my 3rd grade teacher laying out the multiplication tables in front of me, Jesus gave them a great "I am" statement. **THE** way to God. The truth. The life. Every science and every religion has to have a starting point, a foundation, and for me this is it as a Christian. Once I have that fact embedded within me everything else follows. I believe that is precisely what Jesus said in verse 7. I have to get that factual knowledge right. Then, and only then, will I be able to go to the next step and perceive what that means in my life. When I know (factually) who Jesus is, then I will be able to perceive who the Father is and can really know Him.

Jesus told Thomas to get his facts straight and then, only then, would he be able to perceive the whole truth. Jesus the Son and the Father are one. The disciples had spent three years with Jesus the man, and had seen Him do many things. Therefore, they had learned the facts of the case. They had seen Jesus, and, therefore now knew, factually, the Father.

Of course, like many of us, Philip was a little slow putting two and two together. He still wanted to see the Father. I suspect he was still thinking physically and wanted to see with his eyes. Jesus had to restate the obvious one more time. We come to know Jesus the Son in fact, and then, as we put that knowledge into practice, we perceive the truth of who God is. Then He is real in our lives!

<u>Prayer Emphasis:</u>   *Lord, I want to know you, both in fact (head knowledge) and perceptually (heart knowledge). As I study Your Word, show me Jesus, so that I will then really know you.*

MEAN AS A SNAKE

<u>Matthew 10:16</u> *[16] "I am sending you out like sheep among wolves. Therefore be as shrewd as snakes and as innocent as doves."*

Pets! Those adorable animals that we invite into our homes. Do you have a pet or two? What do you picture when pets are mentioned? Those wonderful brown puppy dog eyes staring up at you? That cute little kitten purring softly as it rubs around your ankles? Or maybe it's that mischievous ferret trying to wriggle out of your grasp to see what trouble it can get into.

Whatever the image, many of us greatly enjoy the companionship of our pets. I, for one, have had opportunity to enjoy numerous dogs, but also rescued squirrels, bunnies, and even an opossum and a crow! That opossum had the softest fur I have ever felt, and walking around the yard with a crow sitting on my shoulder attracted lots of strange looks. People have told me I have had some weird pets, but all my pets have added to my enjoyment of the life God put here on this earth. I have even played with some snakes over the years. Yes, snakes!

When you talk about pets I bet you don't picture the hopefully-round (non-poisonous) eyes of a garter snake gazing into yours. More than likely the image you have is that of the python Kaa staring into Mowgli's eyes trying to hypnotize him in Disney's animated **The Jungle Book**. Kaa wasn't trying to be friends with Mowgli; he wanted to eat him!

A former pastor of mine told us he believed too many Christians tend to misread **Matthew 10:16**. They seem to think it says to be mean as a snake and dumb as a bird! I think he was being a little sarcastic, but could there possibly be a hint of truth in his words?

What does the "world" see when they observe Christian behaviors? Do they see highly intelligent people who use their God-given brain for positive purposes? Or do they see people who throw reason to the winds in the guise of "walking in faith" (as if the two actions were in direct opposition)? Does the world see loving people of innocence in whom there is no guile or subterfuge, who can be taken at their word? Or does the world see lemmings simply following the masses off proverbial cliffs, even in the face of multiple warnings?

Is a snake really a shrewd animal? I don't believe they have a large brain, but for such simple creatures they have been in existence for quite a long time. As cold-blooded reptiles, they do know that coiling up on a sunny rock is a very useful activity for their survival. And, despite the image we have of venomous snakes striking unwary walkers, poisonous snakes are more likely to retreat into the undergrowth rather than strike. Most snake bites occur when snakes feel cornered and have no alternative. So, I believe there is some shrewdness in the snake genus.

Actually, considering to whom Jesus is talking, He was probably making more of a spiritual reference to the snake (or serpent, if you prefer) from the Garden of Eden. Ancient peoples tended to think of snakes as creatures of wisdom and cunning. (Again, picture Kaa! But, then again, maybe not!)

So why would Jesus tell His disciples to be like snakes? Are we to emulate the serpent in the Garden trying to deceive Eve? No, God doesn't want us to be deceptive. The serpent was not doing a good thing, but his shrewd wisdom about us frail humans told him this was the way to accomplish his evil goals. So, what are our goals? Or, more correctly, what are Jesus' goals?

In the preceding verses *(10:7-15)* Jesus instructs His disciples and sends them to go and tell their nation the kingdom of heaven has arrived. But He knew that even among their own people this task would be dangerous. The wolves would be out for them. They would need all their intelligence to accomplish their task, but they would also need to avoid deceit. Their innocence needed to be beyond question. The serpent in the garden used his wits to deceive Eve, but he was far from innocent. He used his shrewdness, but with trickery and flattery. Jesus insisted his emissaries emulate His love, not the serpent's guile, while applying all our wisdom to accomplish Jesus' goal.

As I hear Jesus' instructions, we are to tell the world that His Kingdom is near. In this passage He doesn't even use our modern terms of "saving" people or bringing about conversion. The direction is simply to tell. Our associated actions are to minister to the needs of those to whom we are talking, and to give of ourselves. We can do this "giving" because we have received freely from our God. If the one(s) we are sharing with respond to God's call, that is fantastic. If they do not, then simply leave and proceed to share with another.

A simple task? Yes. A dangerous task? Also, yes. Satan, the old serpent, will try every trick in the book to stop us. Do we need wisdom to perform the task? Another yes! But should we be deceitful in our presentation of the message? No, we must be innocent of such trickery if we are to follow our Lord's instructions. The end does not justify the means. Tell what you know. Minister and give from God's bounty, and your Lord will be pleased.

<u>Prayer Emphasis:</u> *Lord, I confess my lack of innocence in my daily Christian walk. May the world about me see from this time on, a person without guile. Grant me your wisdom in determining how to most effectively tell others the blessings of your Kingdom.*

SPIRITUAL OR PHYSICAL?

<u>John 6:51-69</u>   *51 I am the living bread that came down from heaven. Whoever eats this bread will live forever. This bread is my flesh, which I will give for the life of the world."*

...

60 On hearing it, many of his disciples said, "This is a hard teaching. Who can accept it?"

...

66 From this time many of his disciples turned back and no longer followed him.

67 "You do not want to leave too, do you?" Jesus asked the Twelve.

68 Simon Peter answered him, "Lord, to whom shall we go? You have the words of eternal life. 69 We have come to believe and to know that you are the Holy One of God."

Do you like to find familiar shapes in the clouds? Do you see fuzzy bunny rabbits floating overhead, or train engines with steam puffing from their stacks? That can be a fun way to spend a lazy afternoon, but the time will probably not be considered productive, unless you are an artist looking to put your next flight of fancy on canvas.

Have you ever seen, or imagined seeing, a loaf of bread up there? Maybe, but if you have, I suspect you were waiting on a very late lunch and had a grumbly stomach! Now, picture that loaf of bread developing a mouth to speak to you. Or sprouting wings and flying away? It's alive, you might shout, as you tremble inwardly. You had seen a bunny slowly drifting across the sky, or a train engine choo-choo'ing down the tracks. But a loaf of bread with a mind of its own, alive and active? I bet you would be pretty freaked out.

Jesus claimed to be a loaf of living bread that came from heaven. It sorta sounds like the plot of an Indiana Jones adventure, where all the characters are frantically trying to get their hands on that bit of ambrosia or that special morsel that gives everlasting life. Like a drink from the Holy Grail in **Indiana Jones and the Last Crusade**. In fact, Jesus even tells His listeners that if they eat the bread He offers they will live forever. Great!

But, wait a minute. His body is the bread, and Jesus invites them to eat His flesh. This teaching just changed rapidly from a dream come true to a nightmare. I don't believe cannibalism is sanctioned in any modern culture, much less prim and proper first century Judaism. And many of the Jews who had been following Him had that very reaction. *You want us to take a bite out of you*, they may have thought. "That's too hard for us," they told Him. "We can't deal with that."

Note that one of the reasons many of them were with Him at this time was that shortly before they had experienced the feeding of the five thousand *(6:5-13)*. Fantastic! That may have been the biggest and best meal many of them had experienced in months or even years. So, any suggestion of more food would have been very enticing. But this? No, despite the promise of eternal life, they rejected Jesus' words as being too hard, and walked away. They were more concerned about physical life now than about living forever in the future!

This crowd of disciples around Jesus was larger than His special twelve. The ones who gave up on Jesus were not the ones closest to Him, and Jesus understood that. So, He asked His close followers for their thoughts, and, as typical, Peter answered for them. No matter how hard the words were to comprehend, no one else was like Jesus. His very words were life to them because they now believed He had come as God's special Messiah.

What is the difference between the Twelve (close) disciples and the many others gathered around Him who could not accept His latest revelation? Where was their focus? Was it the physical bread and fish and Jesus' body? Couldn't they see that Jesus must not have been talking about literal food, but rather spiritual food? I would think it should have been pretty obvious that Jesus could not have been inviting dozens of followers to descend on Him to bite His fingers, legs, and arms.

The Twelve understood the message as a metaphor, not about literal loaves, but something far more significant, even if less than immediately fulfilling. They made the choice to lift their eyes above the mundane issues of daily existence to see life from God's eyes.

In **Unshakeable Kingdom** Sandi Patty (©1986) sings about how people hear Jesus' words. Many hear Jesus speak of the poor becoming rich and hunger ceasing to be a problem. But Jesus let those people walk away and concentrated on building a more perfect kingdom that can never be destroyed. One that only comes through a close personal relationship with the Christ who loves us as no one else does.

The question for us is how do we hear the words of Jesus? Are we close enough to the Lord to understand His spiritual meaning? Or are we so bogged down in daily survival that we think in purely physical terms? Daily survival is important, and God cares about that too. But God's fervent wish is that we have more, much more.

Prayer Emphasis: *Lord, I confess that simply surviving day-to-day sometimes is all I think about. I know the abundant life you offer is so much more, but life is hard sometimes. As I draw ever closer to you, help me to see life from your eyes.*

ABIDING

John 15: 1-5 *[1] "I am the true vine, and my Father is the gardener. [2] He cuts off every branch in me that bears no fruit, while every branch that does bear fruit he prunes so that it will be even more fruitful. [3] You are already clean because of the word I have spoken to you. [4] Remain in me, as I also remain in you. No branch can bear fruit by itself; it must remain in the vine. Neither can you bear fruit unless you remain in me."*

[5] "I am the vine; you are the branches. If you remain in me and I in you, you will bear much fruit; apart from me you can do nothing."

I have this great doctor I think everyone should know about. You really should start going to see him. He's fantastic! He graduated in 1949, and he really knows his stuff. He's familiar with all the techniques and medicines they used to treat the soldiers in World War II. And he even knows what all the doctors did during the Civil War.

Wait, you say, what about modern medicines and treatments? Well, he hasn't kept up with all those new-fangled things. He doesn't like to waste his time reading things like medical journals. But, what's that I hear you ask, how well do those older treatments work for his current patients? Actually, he hasn't seen any patients in a long time, so I can't tell you much about that. But he assures me he knows what he is doing and can really help people!

Does he collaborate with other physicians and have a well-established treatment facility? No, he says he doesn't need anything like that. But he does have a spare bedroom in his house with lots of clean utensils to use during surgeries. Cuts the cost down, he says, so he can be sure the patient comes first.

So, when can I take you to see him? What do you mean you aren't really interested? He says he is a good doctor and can help you. Isn't that sufficient?

Jesus had some thoughts on the requirements for being able to accomplish a mission, and being well equipped to do so. He shared those thoughts with His disciples the evening before His arrest and crucifixion. Key to those requirements was that His disciples be "up-to-date." For a doctor, that probably means reading those boring medical journals. For a modern engineer it means understanding the benefits of modern computers and studying the latest reports on new scientific discoveries. But what does that mean for a Christian, someone who claims to be a disciple of Jesus Christ?

Before we can answer that question we must understand what it means to claim the name of Christ. To claim to be a doctor, but not see patients and live up to his title, would be nonsense, don't you think? Similarly for a person to claim to be a Christian and not live as one would also make no sense. Jesus told the men gathered around Him that evening that those claiming to be disciples were like branches on a grape vine.

We modern folk often enjoy having pretty plants around us to brighten up our homes, but would you plant a grape vine for its beauty? My memories of grape vines are the thick cords of wood that grew in the woods around my childhood home. Great for swinging on like Tarzan, but not so pretty. No, grape vines are really for one specific purpose. That is to bear grapes. So, if we claim to be Christians and are analogous to branches on a grape vine then we have one specific purpose. That is to bear fruit. In His discourse in John 15 Jesus does not describe specifically what that fruit should be. Rather He concentrates first of all on teaching the disciples that they do have a purpose, bearing fruit.

All farmers know it takes work to make sure their plants actually produce crops. It would be great if you could just throw out seed and come back several months later to gather the produce. But, alas, it doesn't work that way. Similarly, God works on us to help us be productive. Sometimes a branch just proves to be useless and must be discarded. Other times the vine growth must be restrained so that the nourishment goes to the fruit. God does that with us, as well.

Our primary effort as Christians, to be sure God's plans are brought to fruition, is to stay connected to the source of nutrition and power. I don't know about you, but I usually feel pretty inept at leading someone to Christ, or at discipling a new Christian. Sure, I can teach Bible thoughts and tell someone how they should be living, but can I really reach into their soul, touching them deeply and transforming them into Christ-like beings? That seems to require an additional power.

Where does that kind of power come from? For the branches in the analogy (and in all modern vineyards!) it comes from the main vine. If the branch is not attached there is no way for power to flow into and through it. Similarly for Christians, if the Christian is not connected to Christ, there is no way for His power to flow into and through him or her. There would be no grapes maturing on the branches, and no new or maturing Christians sprouting from us. How disappointing that would be!

Remember also that Christ's power is not to make us spectacular branches or to puff us up. I have seen wild grape vines that spread like crazy with branches growing everywhere. But I have never seen those vines bear any fruit worth eating. If we act like those branches and just take nourishment from the vine for our own growth, we will never produce the abundant harvest God desires.

Prayer Emphasis: *Lord, I know I am powerless on my own to bear fruit for Your Kingdom. Prune me, clean me, and remain in me until the harvest. Give me the desire to abide in you forever so that your strength and nourishment will bring forth much fruit.*

SEEING PEOPLE

John 9:1-6   *¹ As he went along, he saw a man blind from birth. ² His disciples asked him, "Rabbi, who sinned, this man or his parents, that he was born blind?"*

³ "Neither this man nor his parents sinned," said Jesus, "but this happened so that the works of God might be displayed in him. ⁴ As long as it is day, we must do the works of him who sent me. Night is coming, when no one can work. ⁵ While I am in the world, I am the light of the world."

⁶ After saying this, he spit on the ground, made some mud with the saliva, and put it on the man's eyes.

Occasionally, I see individuals standing at the entrances to shopping plazas in my small town holding hand-lettered signs. "Need work, please help." "Will work for food." "Need gas money." I do "see" those individuals, but "what" do I see?

Often I see someone to avoid. A panhandler. Someone who wants a handout so they can go buy a drink at the nearest bar. Why don't I see a person who just got laid off from his job and desperately wants to provide for his family? Why don't I see someone who has a minimum wage job and needs to get to the nearest big city to visit their dying mother in the hospital?

Have you ever picked up a hitchhiker? In my youth of the '50s and '60s the answer to that question might very well have been yes, but in this day I suspect the answer for most of us is never. We don't know who that person is. They are probably a serial killer looking for their next victim. Or a carjacker who wants a joyride in my late model SUV. Even if they are standing on the roadside holding a gas can, would you stop and offer a ride? Sometimes we would, but often our fear holds us back, we turn to look a different way, and drive on by, assured that we have prevented another crime!

So, just how do we see people? Or maybe the better question is, **"Do we** see people?" Jesus and His disciples "saw" a man one day, maybe sitting on the roadside in Jerusalem, who was unique. For some unknown reason they already knew his problem, maybe from regularly passing that way. He was blind, obviously I expect, but they also knew that he had not lost his eyesight from disease or an accident. Rather, they knew he had never been able to see. So, what response did they have to this individual and their knowledge?

Why, quite obviously, in the presence of their Master, they thought this was a fine time to discuss deep theology! Leaning on their cultural upbringing, they wanted to learn the reason for the man's distress. For this awful circumstance they believed someone must be to blame. Whose sin had caused his blindness? A very good question, don't you think?

Jesus, as a master of the teachable moment, saw this as a fine opportunity to enlighten His disciples, but I suspect not the way they expected. He did give them a quick, short answer to their question, but did not dwell on the matter of sin's consequences. Instead He showed them what His disciples should do rather than what they should think.

I remember a discussion of this passage written by the Baptist theologian, Herschel Hobbs, in which he noted that the original Greek text from which we have our English translations included no punctuation and even no spaces between words and sentences. Modern translators have to insert proper punctuation to make the English readable. Most translations separate the phrases as seen in the NIV (above), but what if you parse it slightly differently?

Hobbs suggests the first sentence of Jesus' response could be ended with *"**parents sinned.**"* The next sentence then could read *"**But so that the works of God might be displayed in him as long as it is day, we must do the works of him who sent me.**"* Does that change anything? Often I have heard it implied that God caused this blindness from birth so that Jesus could show God's power in a miracle. That could be true, but it causes me some heartburn. Would God really intentionally subject one of His children to physical trauma just to show off His power as an object lesson? That's a hard thought. But if the period Hobbs discusses is moved, that implication is lessened. Instead, the thought seems to become that we are to be involved in doing God's works. Period. While it is day. Whenever and wherever we find opportunity.

So, what did Jesus and the disciples see that day? The disciples saw an object lesson. They saw an opportunity to be "spiritual" and ask a deeply intelligent question from their spiritual Master.

Jesus saw one of His children in severe need. He saw an opportunity to meet a need. Was the spiritual question of the disciples not important? Yes, it was deserving of an answer, which Jesus gave: no one sinned to cause the blindness. And we today need to know that sin is not always the reason for humanity's suffering. But, more importantly in Jesus' eyes, was the lesson the disciples needed to learn about seeing persons, not object lessons, seeing needs, and immediately acting to meet those needs. He knew He had a limited time on earth (His "day"!) and knew He must act while that day lasted. Meeting this man's need was one of the works of His Father who had sent Him. So, Jesus didn't sermonize. He simply acted!

My wife recently wrote a novel about a man who had suffered traumatic brain injury and had difficulty speaking afterward. She used the example of someone "seeing" that man as less than human, an imbecile or retarded. Would that have been Jesus' view? Or would he have seen a man in need of help?

While we are alive on God's earth (our day) we are going to see lots and lots of people, most of them with special needs. Will we see them as God's beloved children? Will we ask deep theological questions about them? Or will we see them as opportunities to actively DO the works of our Father?

<u>Prayer Emphasis:</u>   *Lord, I know that I live in a cynical age that makes me want to isolate from others who might want to hurt me. So, I look away from many in whom I come into contact. Help me to see your children as individuals, and as opportunities to act to meet needs.*

MULTI-PURPOSE TOOLS

Isaiah 44:14-17, 20   *14 He cut down cedars, or perhaps took a cypress or oak. He let it grow among the trees of the forest, or planted a pine, and the rain made it grow. 15 It is used as fuel for burning; some of it he takes and warms himself, he kindles a fire and bakes bread. But he also fashions a god and worships it; he makes an idol and bows down to it.*

16 Half of the wood he burns in the fire; over it he prepares his meal, he roasts his meat and eats his fill. He also warms himself and says, "Ah! I am warm; I see the fire."

17 From the rest he makes a god, his idol; he bows down to it and worships. He prays to it and says, "Save me! You are my god!"...

20 Such a person feeds on ashes; a deluded heart misleads him; he cannot save himself, or say, "Is not this thing in my right hand a lie?"

Over the years we collect many things, but one collection is usually critical to every adult. That is tools. Whether they are tools for car repair, baking bread, or replacing a toilet mechanism, we need our tools. My first tool was a sharp knife to cut apart plastic model parts, but I soon moved up to a screwdriver and some wrenches. Later I needed two sets of wrenches: one English and one metric. Multiple kinds of saws were added, along with needle-nosed pliers and wire cutters. Of course, when I became a home owner I needed a lawn mower and a pair of grass clippers, which later became a lawn **tractor** and a string trimmer. And then, of course, I needed more tools to help repair **those** tools. See the trend? And on and on it went *(and still goes)*.

Many of those tools are designed with a unique purpose in mind. But don't you love it when a single tool can be used for many needs? My go-to multi-purpose tool is a one-inch wide putty knife. It's amazing the way I have used that simple item over the years. I have pushed its slender edge under hard-stuck nails to begin prying them out, used it as an impromptu screwdriver, and scraped caked mud and grass from under my lawn mower. Oh, and I have also actually used it to spread wood putty and caulk!

I don't know how much money I have spent on specialty tools over the years. Many of those have been well worthwhile and saved me lots of distress over how to do certain things. But when I find a multi-purpose tool that I can use over and over, I feel great! I still want that ultimate tool, though. The one I can use for every chore. The one that replaces all my specialty tools? I haven't found it yet!

Isaiah tells us of a man who thought he had found that ultimate tool. This man of Isaiah's time didn't have a car to repair. He didn't need a specialty Bundt cake pan, or a garlic press to season his spaghetti. His needs were much more basic: shelter, warmth from the cold, and a fire to cook his food. But, as all of us eventually realize, he also needed an ultimate purpose and a destination. He needed a god that he could look to beyond his present troubles.

His tool of choice? A cedar, cypress, or oak tree. As you may remember, I told you in another of these devotionals about my love for trees. They are good for so many things: shade from a scorching sun, converting carbon dioxide into oxygen for us to breathe, and for shelter in a pouring rainstorm. And that's just while they are growing. I also like wood furnishings, although that unfortunately means cutting them down. But I can also plant new trees for every one that is cut down.

He could use the wood first to build a shelter to protect himself from rain. He could use scraps and shavings to stoke a fire to warm himself. And that same fire would have been great to roast his meat over. Finally, he could carve leftover pieces into a "god." Pretty smart of him. Right?

Well, maybe not. Most Christians would say how silly! Thinking that chunk of wood, no matter how expertly carved and shaped, could actually be a god? That's just a created object, not the Creator. How can that idol save you? What good would it do to worship that piece of wood?

Think about it, though. Why do we seek or desire a god? We know something is missing from our lives. We know we have needs which we cannot satisfy. Modern Americans may think their needs are better Wi-Fi. Or a fancier automobile. Or a bigger salary. I don't think those things were a concern for someone in the 7th or 8th century BC. He was probably most concerned about survival. How was he going to make it through the next storm? Could he keep from freezing during the coming winter nights when the sun was not shining? Would he be able to fill his belly with meat to give him strength for finding his next meal? Is it not reasonable that he would take advantage of that cedar tree to meet those needs? How big of a stretch is it to go one step further. The cedar can provide shelter, warmth, and cooking. That's almost the ultimate tool. Why can't it also provide even more? Long live the cedar god, he thinks.

Of course, we now know that IS silly. That cedar is not the ultimate tool. There really is no such thing. Right? No, not right. We do have the ultimate tool, although some of you may not like thinking of God as a "tool." I'm not actually calling God a tool. That would be insulting to the God of the Universe, the Creator of all that exists. But in the sense of having that which can solve every dilemma, meet every need, and when all is said and done, take us home with Him to paradise forever, is that not an analogy of "the ultimate tool"?

We may call the wood carver deluded, but how do we fare when we have problems, needs, or weaknesses, and look to money, hard work, prestige, and luck to give us success? Have we really learned anything over the centuries since Isaiah's time?

Prayer Emphasis: *Lord, I know you are not a tool to be purchased at the hardware store, but rather the source of all that exists. Help me remember that when I encounter life's difficulties I have all that I need at my fingertips. Not a tool I make, but the One who exceeds all I can imagine!*

WORKING MY WAY BACK TO YOU

Ephesians 2:8-10 *8 For it is by grace you have been saved, through faith—and this is not from yourselves, it is the gift of God— 9 not by works, so that no one can boast. 10 For we are God's handiwork, created in Christ Jesus to do good works, which God prepared in advance for us to do.*

A favorite singer of mine is Gordon Lightfoot. Most of his work would be considered folk songs, often light-hearted looks at the past, of nature, or simple stories of everyday people. A song called "Rich Man's Spiritual" (Gordon Lightfoot ©1966) rather poignantly tells of a man's desire to get to Heaven when he dies. It's probably not intended to be a theological treatise, but rather, I believe, the thoughts that randomly enter a man's mind as he begins to realize that the day of his demise may be approaching. As you might suspect from the title, this is a man of some means, and probably one who sees heaven as one more place he wants to get to, not necessarily as some great spiritual destination. To him, it is simply the next rest stop on his journey.

What do you believe are the right credentials to enter Heaven? There has to be some key to allow you access. Right? According to the song, the man's first thought is in appearances. If his life looks good, then it must be good. He knows God is not going to let just anyone and everyone in. You need to be a good person, and dirty, stained lives are not going to fit in heaven. Although he probably hasn't been a murderer or thief on Earth, he at least realizes that something a little better is in order. Maybe he just needs to dress up a bit. And being a man of means, why not buy a new **"long white robe"**?

> *I really do believe in Heaven. But how do I get there? I know! If everything looks all right, then I must be all right. All I need for my salvation is for everyone to see me as a good person! Then God will have to accept me into Heaven when I die.*

Doubts begin to slip into his thoughts, however, maybe fearing that God will see past his beautiful covering and want more. Maybe his life needed to be more than just a life of leisure. Some good works would look really good on his resume. He could buy some **"golden slippers"** to show God he really did get out there trying to help people.

> *"But if that doesn't work: I just need to do a few good things during my life (through my own efforts) to make it all right. I can have salvation in heaven if I just work at it a little! If God knows I am trying, then of course He will accept me when I die."*

At this point in the song his thoughts go where those of others have gone. What if his efforts fell short? Buying some **"wings of silver"** from God's heavenly store could be the answer.

> *But in case I just can't seem to do enough, then: I guess I might need some extra help to do more. I will ask God to give me the ability to do additional good works; I probably can't do it all on my*

own anyway. But with God's help I am sure I can work hard enough to be accepted into Heaven.

But then again, his life has primarily been one of ease. Does God want us wealthy folks, or is Heaven a place of rest and promise for those who have suffered on Earth? Maybe he needs to buy himself a **"poor man's troubles."**

> *But what if I can't work my way into heaven? I may need to make some sacrifices. I am sure God will have pity on me because of all the suffering I have had to go through in this life. He will be sure to invite me into heaven when He realizes how hard my life has been and how many earthly sacrifices I have made!*

He now begins to realize that it's just possible that all his efforts (and money!) may go for naught. Everybody needs a little help sometimes. And just maybe he can't buy what he really needs. But, again, he thinks he has the answer. He'll go **"find"** himself **"a smiling angel"**!

> *But what if God doesn't think my life has been hard enough? I may need some expert help. I'll just get my guardian angel to speak up for me. After all, He created those angels to help us, didn't He? God is bound to understand and accept me when I have an angel bring me to Heaven.*

Won't He? After all, who else could I turn to?

Would Scripture help this man in the song? Jesus described the Pharisees as white-washed tombs in **Matthew 23:27**, all beautiful on the outside but full of dead bodies inside. That might have helped him decide the **long white robe** wasn't the answer.

Simon thought he was doing a good thing feeding Jesus a nice dinner in *Luke 7:36-47*, but Jesus noted the act of a sinful woman as being what really had eternal meaning. So, he should realize the **golden slippers** were also inadequate.

Jesus taught a rich young ruler *(Luke 18:18-24)* that all his work was meaningless if his earthly wealth still held sway over him. He needed a new Lord of his life, not **silver wings**.

His parable of a rich man and a poor man named Lazarus (*Luke 16:19-31*) also taught that wealth was not the answer. We can't buy anyone's **troubles** for our own, much less that of a **poor man**. We can't work our way to Him.

And as for help getting to heaven? The man's one correct conclusion is that he needed help. But help from whom? Yes, God's angels are helpers, but the Ephesians verses tells us it is all God's doing. Not his angels and certainly not ours. Yes, we have work to do for our Lord, but nothing to boast about. We can't ever buy our way to Heaven! So, to whom do we turn? Maybe *John 14:6* would help. Jesus said, *"I am the way, the truth and the life."*

Prayer Emphasis: *Lord, teach me that I do have work to do that you prepared in advance for me, not to gain your favor, but rather to emulate my Lord and Savior. Thank you that my entry into your Heaven is by your grace and not something for me to boast about.*

CHRISTIANITY 101

<u>1 John 4:8</u>   *Whoever does not love does not know God, because God is love.*

<u>Mark 12:29-31</u>   *[29] "The most important one," answered Jesus, "is this: 'Hear, O Israel: The Lord our God, the Lord is one. [30] Love the Lord your God with all your heart and with all your soul and with all your mind and with all your strength.' [31] The second is this: 'Love your neighbor as yourself.' There is no commandment greater than these."*

While in college completing my first engineering degree, I took several junior and senior courses that stood out as special. I had previously taken courses in the individual theories of solid mechanics and fluid mechanics. But in the later, advanced classes, I learned that those individual theories could all be derived from the same fundamental equations. Each earlier course was really not unique and separate after all. Amazing! I sometimes thought to myself, why didn't they teach me this first? It would have been helpful to know this before-hand, so I could appreciate those earlier classes more.

Were there reasons for having me take those individual classes first? Could I have really understood the material in my later classes without knowing some basics? It is probably like not teaching calculus to elementary school kids. First, they need to know how to add, subtract, multiply and divide. Then they can understand how to solve algebraic equations in middle school, and finally understand the steps in solving differential equations in college. What a revelation to me!

Can this principle be applied to Christian doctrine? Have you read and/or studied the book of John's Revelations lately? Is there a reason it is the last book of the Bible? And what about that troublesome book of Leviticus? Why is it so near the beginning of the Bible? Do we really need to know not to wear a piece of clothing made out of two different fabrics (**Leviticus 19:19**) in order to understand Revelations? What really does constitute the beginning lessons from God's Word?

I have often noted that the first verse we teach our children is "God is love." Of course, I know a major reason is that it is only three short words. A small child can remember that. (Maybe even an adult!) But there could be another reason. It **IS** the heart of the Gospel. As I see it, everything God has done springs from that. Yes, God is also the Prince of Peace, the Lord of Hosts, a righteous judge, and our eternal Father. But it seems to me that the reason for each of those characters of God is that He IS love. His love for us guides everything He does.

Of course, when we quote that short snippet of scripture, we need to realize we are actually leaving something out. Knowing God means we love. If we don't love, it indicates that we really don't know God, who IS love. Think about it. When asked which was the Greatest

Commandment, Jesus actually listed two. Love the Lord your God, and love your neighbor as yourself. But are they two, or are they actually one, just stated from different perspectives?

John is just making clear what he had heard his Lord say, probably many times, when he wrote "God is love."

So, love is the fundamental concept of Christianity. But how do we know that we are truly loving in the sense of God's love? We know His love from the first chapter of Genesis where He created this wonderful universe just for us, and later when He acted on our behalf by sending Jesus to redeem us back to Him. God is an active God, not just some spiritual being sitting far above us watching the top spin! His love for us always translates into action FOR us.

But how does this revelation about God translate into our lives? John the disciple tells us in his first letter (*1 John 1:6-7*) that if we fellowship with God, then we must walk with Him. John apparently decided this Rabbi had a pretty important message, and he really wanted to learn it. So, Jesus told him to walk with Him. In this case, very literally walk. All around Palestine! If he claimed he wanted fellowship with Jesus, then action had to follow that claim.

First came the acceptance of Jesus as his new Rabbi, immediately followed by the action of walking with Him, and finally, the times of learning from Jesus and growing in that relationship. Sounds like a pretty simple and logical step-by-step process to me.

But getting back to that Leviticus/Revelations thing, how does that fit into the process? John's Revelations are complex and spiritually deep. Maybe that book is one of those senior-level courses. What does that make Leviticus? I don't see a lot of deep spiritual discourse in it. I do see a lot of detailed actions involved. As one of the first books of the Bible, maybe it's like a freshman-level course. What needs to happen right after we commit ourselves to God? According to the example John gave us, we need to act. I believe Leviticus is giving the Israelites (and us) some very specific actions to take which show our commitment to Him as Lord and Savior is real, not shallow "sounds good" words. Maybe we aren't as concerned about the fabrics in our clothes as the Israelites were, but are there other actions we should be taking after becoming Christians?

Once we accept "God is love" we must begin loving as He loves. That means action. *1 John 2:9-10* tells us we cannot claim to be in fellowship with God and hate our brother. We must, not should or might, but must love our brother and even our enemy. Following God's example, that means actions. Not just saying it, but real, visible actions. Jesus' examples of this are best seen in His commendations to the sheep in *Matthew 25*.

As I am writing this in 2021, we are going through a viral pandemic. Americans are sick and dying. In God's eyes, those individuals are our brothers. So, as one specific example, should we not be taking real, physical actions to love them? For me, wearing a mask to prevent viral spread, and getting a vaccine to eliminate possible hosts of the virus are specific actions I can take to care for my brothers and sisters. To do nothing is opposite to the whole concept of God is love.

To be sure, we are talking about actions that come **with** our profession of faith, once we are Christians. These actions happen **because of** our Christianity!

It's like going to college. We commit to a certain school, and then go. There is much to learn while there, and we have to start somewhere. Those freshman-level courses may seem like a pain when we really aspire to be great engineers, accountants, or entrepreneurs. But we have to learn those basic, introductory lessons first. As Christians, we have committed to the God who IS love. I believe our first Christian lesson is to put His love into action. Once we have that one down, watch to see how much more He has to teach us!

Prayer Emphasis: *Lord, I know my commitment to you is only as real as my actions demonstrate. Remind me daily that I must act as if you are Lord. Show me very specific actions I should be taking to love.*

GO FOR THE GUSTO!

<u>1 Corinthians 11:23[b]-26</u> *[23b] The Lord Jesus, on the night he was betrayed, took bread, [24] and when he had given thanks, he broke it and said, "This is my body, which is for you; do this in remembrance of me."*

[25] In the same way, after supper he took the cup, saying, "This cup is the new covenant in my blood; do this, whenever you drink it, in remembrance of me." [26] For whenever you eat this bread and drink this cup, you proclaim the Lord's death until he comes.

Years ago, living in the Hampton Roads area of Virginia, I had a friend named Van who was not really like me at all. I am a bookish type of person, who enjoys studying technical subjects and learning the nuances of math and science. I enjoy being outdoors and doing simple chores, taking hikes in beautiful places, and watching wildlife. My friend never got an advanced education. Van worked as an electrical lineman for years, outside daily doing hard manual work. I don't ever remember seeing him with a book in his hands other than a Bible. Though an outdoorsy-type, I doubt he ever went on a long nature hike.

But he was a fellow Christian who truly loved his Lord. As a hard worker in so many secular day-to-day ways, he also worked hard for

God. As a deacon, he was always dependable and ready to help. Those were the things that brought us together as friends. I'm not sure he regularly understood my perspectives on things, but he always cared. And I appreciated his insights in deacon's meeting discussions. Because we were brothers in our Lord's family, it didn't matter that we were different in so many ways, we were still brothers, and I loved him.

One of the things I remember most from our relationship was how he took the Lord's supper. Our church at the time had one tradition that many other churches might see as unusual. The bread used was not the common small bit of cracker or a stiff wafer. Instead, for many years they had a local bakery prepare them round loaves of egg-bread for the service. Yes, I know it was not yeast-free as most churches use, but it served a unique purpose that has stuck with me for long after. The pastor would take the bread and, after reading Scripture, often including **Matthew 26:26**, he would pick up the loaf and break it in half, noting that the bread, like Jesus' body, was broken for us. That symbolism makes the images of Christ being beaten, crucified, and finally pierced with a spear very vivid to me. It could, and should, have been me, but instead my Lord voluntarily took my punishment. Like the bread, Jesus' body was broken for me!

After the bread was broken, the deacons serving the supper passed it throughout the congregation for everyone to break off a piece for themselves. Many individuals would simply take a small pinch. Others might take a little bigger piece that they could taste. But not Van! When the loaf came to him, he would grab a handful. Sometimes I worried how much would be left for others.

Asked one time about this behavior, Van explained that if Christ was willing to give so much of Himself for us, he wanted to take everything God had to offer! Jesus was not a timid person, and neither was Van. For him, the Supper observance was an opportunity for him to identify with his Lord. Were his actions appropriate? Was Van overacting and/or being rude by grabbing a handful of bread during the Supper?

I enjoy live music and relish sitting in the concert hall listening to talented musicians. While doing so I have observed lots of people reacting to an excellent performance at a concert's finale. Some jump up quickly and applaud enthusiastically, maybe including a few "hoots and hollers." Others smile and clap vigorously while remaining seated, and still others simply smile and sit still with only a few claps. Are some of them wrong-headed and unappreciative? Are others rude and overbearing? I think not. They are simply responding as becomes who they really are and how God made them.

How do you respond when God speaks to you? In worship, do you simply revel in His presence? Or do you jump up and lift your hands to

Him? When He calls you to go somewhere in His service, you may call on friends to immediately pray. Or you may simply offer your hands to Him without fanfare and work behind the scenes to serve your fellow man. I really don't believe either is right or wrong. The main point is to respond.

When we accept Him as Lord and Savior, we claim to truly believe in and follow Him. Are we ready to jump in feet-first with all our being and proclaim His message until He returns?

Who did God make you to be? God made Van to be a man of action who wanted to experience all that God had to offer. So, he chose to "go for the gusto" in his participation in the Lord's Supper. You may have a calmer disposition that savors your Lord's work in your life more contemplatively. Or your personality may lie somewhere between those two extremes. No right or wrong response. Simply acknowledge that you are His, and act as He directs.

You can still take a small pinch of communion bread. Or feel free to grab a large chunk. But regardless, enjoy your time with Him. Take all He has to offer you, and revel in His love.

Prayer Emphasis: *Lord, you made me in Your image, but also as a unique individual. Show me how to use that personality in ways that glorify you, and to experience you fully.*

<h1 style="text-align:center">Scripture Cross-reference:</h1>

Reference	Page
Genesis 1:31	28
Leviticus 19:18	29
Leviticus 19:19	93
1 Samuel 16:7	28
2 Chronicles 32:24-25	21
2 Chronicles 33:1-2	19
2 Chronicles 33:12	19
2 Chronicles 34:2	22
Psalms 1:1-3	55
Isaiah 44:14-17,20	84
Ezekiel 37:1-14	24
Matthew 5:21-22	32
Matthew 5:43-45a	29
Matthew 10:16	67
Matthew 10:7-15	69
Matthew 19:26	25
Matthew 23:27	27, 90
Matthew 25	95
Matthew 26:26	98
Matthew 28:6	39
Mark 9:21-24	47
Mark 10:17-22	33
Mark 12:29-31	92
Luke 7:36-47	91
Luke 9:23	36
Luke 10	30
Luke 11:34	28
Luke 16:19-31	91
Luke 18:18-24	91
John 6:51-69	71
John 6:5-13	72

Reference	Page
John 9:1-6	79
John 14:3-9	63
John 14:6	91
John 15	45
John 15:1-5	75
John 15:5	50
John 15:8	58
John 19:28	39
John 19:30	39
Acts 9:10-13	43
Romans 11:33	12
1 Corinthians 9:19-23	59
1 Corinthians 11:23b-26	97
1 Corinthians 12:7-10	54
1 Corinthians 12:12-14	51
1 Corinthians 12:15-26	33
1 Corinthians 12:18	53
2 Corinthians 8:9	11
2 Corinthians 9:10	15
Galatians 5:13	59
Ephesians 2:8	11
Ephesians 2:8-10	88
1 Peter 4:11	15
1 John1:6-7	94
1 John 2:9-10	95
1 John 4:8	92

ABOUT THE AUTHOR

Ken Tatum is a retired aerospace engineer who has taught adult Bible studies for 40+ years. He grew up in the Bible Belt city of Nashville where he got an excellent Bible background, reading a chapter every night with his family. Accepting Christ as Savior at age 11 he was confident in his salvation, but was not deeply committed to Him as Lord. As a young married man he was led to take a position teaching his Sunday School class after the previous teacher left, and has not stopped teaching since. Partly he felt called to it and partly he learned so much more teaching than as a student. Later experiences in Master Life, Prayer Life, and Experiencing God classes (both taking and teaching) led him into a richer and more rewarding relationship with his Lord. He was called to a day-to-day job as an engineer, but has received the most joy teaching Scripture and awareness of beliefs of cults and other world religions. His wife Diane has been his constant encourager, and his extended family of two sons, two daughters-in-law and four grandsons are continual blessings.

NOTES

Look for books by:

Diane E. Tatum
Christian Romance: Contemporary, History, & Mystery

Visit Diane Tatum at:

www.dianeetatumwriter.com

Author Page at: amazon.com/author/dianeetatum

Latest Release:

Hiding in the Highlands

Look for all her books on Amazon:

Gold Earrings
Mission Mesquite

Colonial Dream:

Main

A Time to Fight
A Time to Love
A Time to Choose

Main Street Mysteries:

#1 Kudzu Sculptures
#2 Gemini Conspiracy
#3 Attic Visitations
#4 DNA Secrets
#5 The Disappearing Diaspora - Coming in May 2022!

Romancing the Billionaire: Oxford Fairy Tale
MISSletoe Romance: Dreaming of a Wedded Christmas
Never Mind Time: Cecilia's Y2Key

An Unordinary Romance: Finding Love in the Fog of Aphasia

<u>Watch for:</u>

Kate's B & B with the Bell Witch
Colonial Dream: Book 4 *A Time to Create*